the WINE
LOVER'S
DRINK
BOOK

John J. Poister

COLLIER BOOKS
MACMILLAN PUBLISHING COMPANY
NEW YORK

COLLIER MACMILLAN PUBLISHERS
LONDON

Macmillan Publishing Company
866 Third Avenue, New York, N.Y. 10022
Collier Macmillan Canada, Inc.

Library of Congress Cataloging in Publication Data
Poister, John J.
The wine lover's drink book.
Includes index.
1. Wine and wine making.   2. Alcoholic beverages.
I. Title.
TX951.P57   1983   641.2'22   83-15265
ISBN 0-02-010090-6

10   9   8   7   6   5   4   3   2   1

Designed by Jack Meserole

Printed in the United States of America

*To my editors, with special
thanks to Robert A. Fitz
and Louise Gault, who shared
my belief that wine drinks
as much as wine drinking
would become a part of the
American way of life.*

CONTENTS

Madeira ★ *A selection of the best recipes, old and new, encountered during world travels including lesser-known jewels of the Mediterranean such as Marsala, Terragona, and Moscato* ★ *Dispelling old-fashioned ideas concerning the use of fortified wines*

INTRODUCTION

In the beginning there was wine.

No one really knows when man first began to make wine, for the answer is shrouded in the mists of prehistory. Some archaeologists believe that grapes were first trod at least ten thousand years ago, and it is very likely that wine made from palms, dates, and fermented honey came even earlier.

The Mesopotamian peoples who migrated to the plains of the Tigris and Euphrates rivers were enjoying the pleasures of the grape in 4000 B.C. Since grapes were not native to this area, the art of the vine must have come from another land and from an earlier time. All of the great ancient civilizations cultivated the grape and made wine. The Egyptians believed that Osiris bestowed wine upon mankind as a gift, and the Greeks worshipped Dionysus, son of Zeus and god of wine, who first brought wine to the lips of mortals.

There are frequent references to wine in the Bible, and the book of Genesis credits Noah with being the very first viticulturist (Genesis 9:20). One of the first punch drinks is described by Daniel in his account of a dinner given for four hundred guests by Belshazzar, the king of Babylon. In addition to red wines, there was also served "a heady brew of barley and a wine of date palms stiffened with honey" (Daniel 5:1).

As André Simon observed in one of his many distinguished writings on wine, "Man first learned to make his wine aromatic when he discovered that by adding honey or sage or some herb to his sour wine, it became more palatable." Thus the epoch of wine drinks began with the very beginnings of civilization.

While purists are understandably inclined to look with disdain on the use of additives of any kind in wine, the fact of the matter is that the modern vintner is faced with the same problem as his Greek counterpart of two thousand years ago: how best to preserve the vintage. This challenge explains some of the more bizarre wine mixtures of the ancients. The early Greek vintner used sweet hepsema (wine must, reduced by boiling, until it becomes sweet) and honey to mellow his wine during fermentation. Since spoilage was a severe problem, he would often add resin or pine-gum to extend the life of the wine. In ancient Greece even the mouths and lids of wine jars were covered with pine pitch to aid in the preservation of the wine. The practice of resinating wine persists in Greece to this day, and the pronounced taste of pine pitch is to be found in most popular Greek table wines.

A variety of substances were used for clearing the wine (*fining*), and also as preventives against spoilage. Ground seashells, baked salt, ashes, chalk, burnt gall nuts and acorns, cedar cones and olive pits are mentioned in early Greek writings. Since salt acted as a preservative, sea water was widely used to prevent wine from turning sour, and a form of mulling of the wine was occasionally performed with a burning pine torch or a red-hot iron. Done not for aesthetic purposes, this was rather a primitive attempt at sterilization of the undesirable bacteria that "turned" the wine.

The ingenuity of the Greeks came to the fore in the matter of flavored wine mixtures. A popular practice was steeping flower blossoms of many kinds in wine; among the most frequently mentioned botanicals were clover, saffron, sweet flag, spikenard, myrtle berries, cedar, and bitter almond. Hippocrates, the father of medicine, is credited with originating a recipe that called for the use of wine sweetened with honey and flavored with cinnamon. In its various forms, this potion became known as *hippocras* and was a popular drink of the Middle Ages.

There are repeated references in Homer's writings to blended wines. In the *Iliad*, Homer describes a feast given by Nestor, who had recently returned from doing battle with the Trojans. Hekamede, a lady of the house, prepared a punch using Pramian wine, supposedly very heavy and sweet, not unlike a ruby port, which was popular among the Greeks as a base for mixed drinks. The punch was prepared with a good lacing of grated goat's-milk cheese and a generous sprinkling of barley on the top, and served with a raw onion—which was to be eaten with the drink.

A happy pastime in ancient Greece was the *symposium*—not a serious affair dealing with weighty matters, but simply a good old-fashioned drinking party. The symposium (the word means "drinking together") usually moved into high gear after the food had been consumed. Then the wine began to flow. The strength and the quantity of the flow was regulated by the *symposiarch*, the progenitor of the modern-day toastmaster, who presided over the festivities and oversaw the diluting of the wine with water: Presumably, if things got out of hand, he could elect to shut off the flow of wine to the revelers or increase the amount of water in the wine from, say, half and half, to one part wine to three parts water.

The Greeks enjoyed the physical pleasures of life and liked having their wine drinks "on the rocks"—when rocks were available, of course. There are accounts of wine being mixed with cold spring water and poured into containers packed with ice. On very special occasions, slaves were dispatched to the mountains to fetch snow, which would be served with the wine in drinking cups. The apparent popularity of this "Greek Mist" suggests that tastes for some things, at least, have not changed drastically in the past several thousand years.

When it came to imaginative drink mixing, the Romans easily put the rest of the world of classical antiquity to shame. The ingenuity and daring of their innovations knew no bounds: Roman wines were infused with a plethora of substances that truly boggle the mind. The arsenal of ingredients used to assault Roman wines included asafoetida, aloes, anise, myrrh, myrtle, pepper, bitumen, camomile, violets, rose petals, poppies, honey, mastic gum, marjoram, spikewood, rosemary, marble dust, boiled sea water, hyssop, worm-wood, cypress gums, pitch, tar, almonds, chalk, salt, saffron, a variety of flower essences, fruits, perfumes, and even pigeon's dung.

Some Roman wines were apparently subjected to a heat treatment, as is done today in the making of Madeira. This process took place in *fumaria*, kilnlike ovens, where the wines developed a smoky flavor. This smoky quality is referred to in many early writings. Horace, speaking of "smoked Falernians," a popular Roman wine of that period, poetically observes, "We'll pierce a glass with mellow juice replete, mellowed with smoke since Tully ruled the state." Pliny, reflecting the attitudes of more enlightened vintners, wrote, "Wines matured by age and not by smoke are the most wholesome."

The patrician palate was conditioned to the use of aromatics in both food and wine. Favorite Roman wine drinks were *piperatum*, made with honey and pepper; *mulsum*, a mixture of wine and honey that was added to table wines; *melitites*, a combination of must (unfermented grape juice), salt, and honey that was also mixed with table wines; and *absinthites*, which consisted of wine and wormwood—possibly the forerunner of vermouth.

As Roman culture and customs spread throughout Europe with Caesar's legions, vineyards were established, and the methods of making and flavoring wine that had been started by the Greeks became common knowledge to the very ends of the Roman Empire. The Roman influence persisted during the Middle Ages, for the practice of spicing wine was universal. Hippocras, known by other names, such as *piment* in medieval Britain, was nevertheless basically a mixture of wine and sugar or honey and spices. It was the common drink of the day. Popular later in Georgian England, the basic formula still survives in *Glühwein* and many other similar wine drinks.

Riding tandem with man's irresistible desire to flavor his wine cup down through the ages has been the unending struggle to preserve wine from becoming prematurely undrinkable. It is entirely possible that the first interesting flavor innovations were the result of prehistoric man's efforts to save his wine. Some of the oldest recorded methods of preserving wines are still in use today. We may recoil at the Roman practice of pouring plaster into wine, but the very same procedure is followed today in Spain, where gypsum is added to sherry to increase its acidity. And Elizabethans added lime to wine to keep it from going bad—a practice still carried out in some parts of eastern Europe and the Middle East. There are endless references in old English books on food and drink to methods of doctoring wines. Sometimes beef was thrown into the wine during the fermentation period, and depending upon the length of the fermentation process, one could, no doubt, have wine rare, medium, or well done. The more accepted Renaissance practice of enhancing (or in the case of poor wine, disguising) the flavor of wine was—in addition to or in place of the usual spice treatment—to steep wine with various flower blossoms. Present-day German *Maiwein*, known everywhere as May wine, a white wine infused with *Waldmeister* (which we know as the aromatic herb, woodruff), is a delightful hand-me-down from the Dark Ages.

It may come as a shock to some wine connoisseurs to learn that even the most revered château bottlings are treated with additives in deference to the demands of world popularity. Wine must be robust in order to ship well. Sulphur dioxide is commonly used to subdue unwanted bacteria that interference with the function of the wine yeasts. Sugar is frequently added to wines to increase the alcoholic content, and tannin and tartaric acid are used to give a wine greater longevity. Some rosé wines are even dyed with cochineal, the dried bodies of female scale insects, to give them better color.

The modern-day vintner has at his disposal more than sixty different inhibitors, stabilizers, modifiers, preservatives, and other additives to aid him in his primary mission: getting the vintage to market in the greatest quantity and in the best possible condition. The use of additives is usually executed with great care and is strictly regulated in all major wine-growing countries, but if you want your wine straight, you had better make it yourself and drink it while it is very young.

So, fellow wine lover, when your favorite aunt offers you a tall, cool claret lemonade on a sultry summer afternoon, don't hastily turn aside your highly educated palate. Drink the offering and be grateful. After the wine has withstood a dousing with chemicals, albeit expertly administered, what harm can a little lemon and sugar do?

*　　*　　*

Let us now give thought to a brighter, more pleasurable side of wine mixtures. Apart from the never-ending need to conserve the pride of the vintner's skill, and the bizarre tastes of another age, the product of man's experimentation with various wine mixtures through the years has yielded some rich treasures. They are the great heritage of drinks based upon wine. Some of these formulations have become true classics. Others may be near-classics, but have not quite reached the mark, in my opinion at least. Here follows a wide range of wine drinks for every taste and persuasion; some are curiosities, most are satisfying, all are interesting and worthy of thoughtful consideration by anyone who enjoys wine.

A Note on Names

There is considerable curiosity regarding the origin of drink names. Where do they come from? What is their significance, if any? In days past, it was not unusual to name a food dish or a drink concoction to commemorate a notable event such as a coronation, the winning of a battle, an anniversary, or a wedding. Many drinks, specialties of a famous hotel, club, or restaurant, were given the names of the establishment, and well-known or loyal customers were honored by having drinks created and named for them. Operas, Broadway shows, and stars of stage and screen have often been recipients of this tribute.

Most mixer's manuals are silent on the origins of the drinks they contain, and we can only speculate on their provenance. Some names, such as those alluding to places, are self-explanatory. There is scarcely a major city in the world that has not been recognized by being incorporated into the name of a cocktail. And, of course, there are the drinks whose names were obviously coined for the purpose of attracting attention and curiosity. Anyone can create a special drink and tag it with a name. If you happen upon a mixed drink that is particularly appealing, do as so many others have done—adapt it for your own tastes and name it for yourself.

the WINE LOVER'S DRINK BOOK

I | A DISTINGUISHED WINE DRINK SAMPLER

What makes a "classic" wine drink? The answer, of course, is a recipe endowed with those qualities that characterize anything classic—whether it be an automobile by Bugatti, a painting by Picasso, or a recording by Louis Armstrong from the 1920s. Basically a classic is a benchmark creation against which all prior or subsequent efforts of a similar nature are compared. Age, originality, and popularity are important factors, but definitely secondary considerations.

Thus it is with drink recipes. In the following pages I have arbitrarily selected twenty-nine unique wine drink formulations. Some are recent, some are ancient, and some may even be considered cliché concoctions by the more sophisticated swiggers among us. Most are tasty, a few may even seem insipid (only because they are not in vogue with today's swing to lightness and dryness), but all are benchmark formulations that set the style for countless variations and similar inventions. Among many thousands of drink recipes extant, these few are the pacesetters from which were generated countless taste-alikes—some of which were improvements and others of which were decidedly not. The creative process is a dynamic one, and just as modern masterpieces are, perhaps at this very moment, being created in all areas of human activity, so it is with the heady world of wine drinkery. At any moment a new drink formulation may appear on the scene to provide inspiration for a wave of similar libations to titillate the public palate and satisfy the desire for new taste sensations.

Further, in this chapter we will consider wine drink recipes chosen to exemplify imaginative and, in some cases, ingenious blending of tasteful ingredients. In many cases these drinks, in my opinion, qualify for the designation "near-classics," and at the very least must be regarded as "standards," since nearly all have held up against the ravages of time and vacillating tastes. But more important, I think you will agree that all of these wine drink recipes, if properly handled, make damn good drinks.

Please note that all recipes are for one serving unless otherwise specified.

The first of our classic twenty-nine is an ancient recipe of Sicilian origin that is quite possibly the great-grandfather of all the wine-and-egg mixtures, of which there are many. *Zabaione* or *Zabaglione* is simply egg yolk, sugar, and Marsala, a strong, sweet, aromatic wine grown around the Sicilian seaport of the same name. One old recipe specifies that the amount of wine to each egg yolk is to be precisely that amount of liquid displaced by the egg before it is broken. Sugar is a matter of taste, and the amount is related to the sweetness of the wine being used.

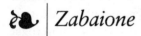 | *Zabaione*

3 egg yolks
3 tbsp. sugar
4 oz. Marsala

Beat egg yolks and sugar with a whip and blend in Marsala. Cook in a double boiler, stirring constantly. When the mixture thickens to the desired consistency, remove and serve in small cups or goblets. This "drink" is eaten with a spoon.
SERVES 2.

A DISTINGUISHED WINE DRINK SAMPLER

Glühwein is another hot, spiced wine drink of ancient lineage. It can be made in many ways, using a variety of wines. Madeira is especially bracing on a cold winter night after a day on the ski slopes.

❧ | *Glühwein*

1 fifth Malmsey Madeira
Peel from 1 lemon and 1 orange
2 or 3 cinnamon sticks, broken
2 or 3 whole cloves
⅓ of a whole nutmeg, cracked
Honey to taste

Heat wine in a saucepan with fruit peels, cinnamon sticks, cloves, and nutmeg. Add honey, stirring to make sure it is dissolved. Bring mixture to a simmer and serve in preheated ceramic mugs.
SERVES 6.

The *Posset*, an old English invention and a most nourishing drink, is basically a mixture of hot wine, milk, and spices. Eggs were often used, in combination with the milk or by themselves, and ale can be substituted for wine or used in combination. A modern variation:

❧ | *Egg Posset*

6 egg yolks
½ cup sugar or to taste
½ tsp. cinnamon
½ tsp. nutmeg
½ tsp. cloves
1 quart dry red or white wine

Beat egg yolks well with sugar and spices. Heat wine in a saucepan, bring to a simmer, and pour into egg mixture slowly, stirring constantly. Serve in preheated cups.
SERVES 6.

Cobblers were the rage when Grandmother was very young and can be made with either wines or various kinds of spirits. The *Sherry Cobbler* was especially popular at the turn of the century. There are many variations to this recipe. If a sweet sherry is used, omit the sugar syrup and use more curaçao. Some recipes call for the use of a tea-spoon of orange or lemon juice. Here is a basic recipe:

⟨● | *Sherry Cobbler*

Dash of pineapple or plain sugar syrup
Dash of curaçao
Dash of lemon or orange juice (optional)
4 oz. medium sherry
Pineapple stick, lemon peel, and sprig of mint (optional)

Fill a 12-oz. Collins glass three quarters full of finely shaved ice, add pineapple syrup, curaçao, citrus juice if desired, then sherry. Mix briskly with a bar spoon until outside of glass is frosted. Garnish with a pineapple stick, a twist of lemon peel, and a sprig of mint.

The mulling of wine is a practice dating back to antiquity. In the Middle Ages it was a common custom to douse wine with herbs, spices, and sugar. Since sugar was expensive, it was reserved for the privileged; the ordinary citizen had to make do with honey. Tankards of wine were then mulled with a hot poker, which undoubtedly imparted a toasty flavor. Present-day mulling is performed with more gentility, in a saucepan. Whether or not this refinement is an improvement or merely a convenience is open to question. This Elizabethan recipe for *Mulled Claret* can be executed by the hearth or on the range. In view of the shortage of hot pokers in the service of mulling drinks, we have chosen the latter method.

❧ | Mulled Claret

3 oz. dry red Bordeaux
1 oz. port
¾ oz. brandy
Pinch of cinnamon
Pinch of cloves
Pinch of nutmeg
Lemon peel

Warm all ingredients in a covered saucepan until piping hot—but don't boil. Serve with a thin slice of lemon peel in a preheated ceramic mug.

A modern version of *Mulled Claret* with liqueur and egg is this piquant *potpourri*, which was a popular American drink of the 1890s.

❧ | The Locomotive

6 oz. Burgundy or
   Bordeaux
½ oz. curaçao
½ oz. maraschino liqueur
Pinch of cinnamon
2 or 3 whole cloves
1 oz. honey
1 egg, lightly beaten
Lemon slice

Combine wine, liqueurs, spices, and honey in a saucepan over medium heat. When honey has dissolved, stir in the egg and bring to a simmer. Serve in a preheated ceramic mug and garnish with lemon slice.

The *Black Velvet*, a jewel among wine drinks, was very popular in Victorian England. This perfect union of champagne and stout produces a true taste sensation that never fails to astonish anyone trying the mellow mixture for the first time. Make sure that the ingredients are well chilled and that the goblets that are used have been refrigerated at least an hour before serving time.

❧ | Black Velvet

6½ oz. (split) champagne
Equal portion of Guinness
   stout

Pour gently, and simultaneously, into a large, prechilled goblet.

The *French 75* certainly qualifies as a classic wine drink, if for no other reason than that it is well known throughout the land. What is not so well known is the correct recipe. A proper French 75 is not, as many suppose, a mixture of gin and champagne. It is, rather, a traditional marriage of cognac and champagne named by American doughboys during World War I to honor the redoubtable French army field piece with a bore diameter of 75 millimeters. If you have a yen for gin and champagne, well and good, but don't call it a French 75, for gin (London dry gin, that is) is an English invention and is not native to France or French drinking habits.

❧ | The French 75

Juice of half a lemon or 1
   lime
½ tbsp. of sugar syrup or to
   taste
2 oz. cognac
Brut champagne

Place several ice cubes in a 12-oz. Collins glass, add juice, sugar syrup, and cognac, stir well with a bar spoon, and fill glass to the brim with chilled champagne.

The French 75 is also known, with minor modifications, as the *Maharajah's Burra Peg*, the *King's Peg*, and the *Russian Cocktail*.

These variations are all mixtures of champagne and cognac, *sans* lemon and sugar. The Russian Cocktail is differentiated from the others by a dash of Angostura Bitters.

The combination of champagne and fruits offers endless opportunities for zesty, refreshing drinks, ideally suited to brunches and before-noon tippling. Champagne and orange juice is an old favorite. In the early twenties at Buck's Club in London, a preluncheon drink known as *Buck's Fizz* was very popular; it was made with one part orange juice, two parts champagne, and a teaspoon of grenadine. A similar drink, *sans* grenadine, is served at the Ritz Bar in Paris. They call it *Mimosa*, but I personally like to call it

❧ | *The Park Avenue Orange Blossom*

Juice of 1 orange
Champagne, medium dry

Pour orange juice into a 12-oz. Collins glass with cracked ice and fill with champagne or mix it without ice in a large chilled wine goblet. Proportions are approximately two parts champagne to one part orange juice, but may be varied according to your taste.

The idea of mixing a white and a red wine together, while revolting to some wine drinkers, nevertheless has many devotees, to judge by the popularity of *Cold Duck*—a mixture of sparkling white and red wines. Like all fads that pop up from nowhere and climb to meteoric heights, the Cold Duck idea is not new, but simply recycled. Many years ago, a drink known as *Turkish Blood*, consisting of half champagne and half red Burgundy, was making the rounds. If you like to drink mixed wines, I suggest you buy only cheap domestic wines for this exercise.

🐦 | Cold Duck

1 fifth champagne
1 fifth sparkling Burgundy

Mix well-chilled wines gently in a pitcher and serve in chilled champagne glasses. You may add slices of orange or lemon peel if you wish.
SERVES 12.

Sangría, in its many forms, is a prime example of a simple, refreshing, and very satisfying wine drink. While basically a combination of oranges, lemons or limes, sugar, and red or white wine, there are versions that specify the use of various fruit syrups, liqueurs, and spirits, such as gin, vodka, and brandy. In making the basic, and perhaps the most common recipe, the fruits may be used in two ways. Some prefer to heat the juice from lemons and oranges, along with some of the peel from each, in sugar syrup. Sometimes a stick of cinnamon or some allspice is added. This mixture is then cooled, strained, and poured into a pitcher of chilled red wine and garnished with fresh fruit slices. Another, simpler, method calls for mixing fruit juices, peels, and syrup in a pitcher of red wine without any prior preparation. Club soda may be added if desired.

🐦 | Sangría

1 fifth dry red wine
Juice of 1 orange
Juice of 1 lemon or 2 limes
4 oz. sugar syrup to taste
2 oz. curaçao or Grand
   Marnier (optional)
1 pint club soda (optional)

Prepare according to one of the methods described above. Serve in a pre-chilled pitcher. Ice cubes may be added if the weather is hot. Add several ounces of curaçao or Grand Marnier if you wish.
SERVES 6.

For the colder climes, where hot drinks are a necessity, the Swedes have devised a potent restorative called *Glögg*. The word *glögg* means "glow" in Swedish; thus the name is appropriate, because glögg is flamed with sugar cubes in a ladle or on a rack over the punch bowl for Christmas and other festive occasions. The name also describes the feeling that creeps over you after you have had your second cup. There are many variations of this popular drink, and in Sweden nearly everyone has his or her own favorite recipe for adding various spices and spirits to red wine.

૨ત | *Glögg*

1 fifth dry red wine
1 fifth aquavit or vodka
1 cup blanched almonds
1 cup raisins
2 cinnamon sticks
1 orange peel, studded with cloves
12 cardamom seeds
10 to 12 sugar cubes

Place all ingredients except sugar in a covered container and let steep for several hours; heat and pour mixture into a flameproof punch bowl. Just before serving to guests, place sugar cubes in a ladle with a little glögg and ignite. Continue dipping ladle into glögg and pouring flaming liquid back into the bowl until sugar is dissolved. Extinguish flames with a cover and ladle into cups with a portion of almonds and raisins, which may be eaten with a spoon.
SERVES 12.

A word of caution: Don't let the flames burn overly long lest the life of your party go up in smoke.

* * *

What *Jul Glögg* is to Sweden, the *Wassail Bowl* is to England. Traditionally, it is made with wine or ale, alone or in combination; some old recipes specify cider. This Elizabethan recipe is typical:

❧ Wassail Bowl

1 cup sugar
1½ tsp. grated nutmeg
6 whole allspice berries
1 tsp. powdered ginger
6 cloves
1 cinnamon stick
½ tsp. mace
2 fifths Madeira
6 eggs, separated
4 baked apples, cored but not skinned
4 oz. cognac (optional)

Boil sugar and spices together in a cup of water until all sugar is dissolved. Reduce heat, add wine, and simmer over low heat, *but don't boil*. Beat egg yolks and whites separately; fold together. Add small amounts of beaten eggs to wine mixture, stirring constantly. Just before serving, add apples which have been cored, but not skinned, and baked with sugar, powdered cinnamon, ginger, and nutmeg. The wassail bowl itself should be preheated to keep wine mixture hot. Cognac adds a little extra snap.
SERVES 10 TO 12.

The combination of the damp, dreary English climate and the irrepressible English spirit have caused the birth of more drink recipes than any phenomenon except Prohibition. During the greater part of the year, hearty elixirs are positive necessities for the maintenance of a sound mind, and in many instances required for the preservation of health, and perhaps even life itself. This was dramatically demonstrated during a grouse-shooting expedition with some English friends near Kinnloch Rannoch, Perthshire, early one cold, blustery, soaking-wet November. (After all, who really would want to be in Scotland in November? Only an Englishman, who doesn't care about the weather, or an American, who doesn't know any better.) Upon our return from the high moors one howling night, palsied, blue, and waterlogged, we were offered this time-honored restorative at the Dunalastair Hotel. Soon things were put right.

Samuel Johnson maintained that "claret . . . is for boys, port for men, but he who aspires to be a hero must drink brandy." Apparently, he had no doubts concerning his qualifications for the last two categories, for he dearly loved his port and adored his brandy, and frequently drank them together. The *English Bishop* was surely invented for the likes of Samuel Johnson.

ᔏ | *English Bishop*

1 large, choice orange
Brown sugar
Whole cloves
1 fifth port
1 large cinnamon stick
 (optional)
4 oz. cognac

Wet the orange with a little water, score lightly in a crisscross or diamond pattern, roll in brown sugar, stud with cloves, and place under the broiler. Pour port into a saucepan with a little additional brown sugar; if desired, add cinnamon stick; bring to a simmer. When orange is slightly brown and heated through, quarter it and add to wine. Pour in cognac just before serving. SERVES 6.

The *Syllabub* (sometimes spelled *Sillabub* or *Sillibub*) is a very old recipe, which either may be taken as a drink or served as a dessert. There are many recipes extant—all very rich and sweet—utilizing, in addition to sherry, port, Madeira, and white dessert wines such as sauterne.

ᔏ | *The Syllabub*

1 fifth cream sherry
3 cups heavy cream
3 cups milk
1½ cups castor (superfine)
 sugar to taste
Nutmeg (optional)

Beat ingredients, except nutmeg, well and serve in sherbet or champagne saucers. Grate a little nutmeg on top, if you wish.
SERVES ABOUT 24.

The *Negus* is a hot, sweet wine drink, made with or without spices and named in honor of Col. Francis Negus, an English luminary who lived during the reign of Queen Anne. It is usually made with port or sherry, but the colonel's favorite recipe called for white wine "made hot and sweetened." He was in the habit of drinking this after his morning's walk.

è❧ | *Negus*

1 fifth port	Heat port and place in a warmed
6 sugar cubes	pitcher. Take sugar cubes and carefully
Lemon peel	rub the zest (outside yellow coloring of
1 cinnamon stick (optional)	the peel) from a lemon and add sugar
6 whole cloves (optional)	cubes to wine. Pour in 2 cups of boiling
Grated nutmeg (optional)	water and add spices if desired. Some
Lemon juice (optional)	also prefer to squeeze in a little lemon
	juice.
	SERVES 6 TO 8.

Wine flips, like similar recipes involving eggs, are both food and drink. Their long-standing popularity is justified. Best known is the classic *Sherry Flip*.

è❧ | *Sherry Flip*

2 oz. sherry	Shake all ingredients, except nutmeg,
1 tsp. sugar	with cracked ice; strain and serve in a
1 egg	chilled whiskey sour glass with a little
Freshly grated nutmeg	grated nutmeg on top.

There is hardly a more festive or satisfying way to enjoy wine than to sip a succulent punch mixture among good friends all gathered 'round the flowing bowl. There are so many fine punch recipes in existence that it is difficult to select a single recipe that can be called a "classic." It is more accurate to say that the recipes given here are simply representative of a genre of carefully concocted wine drinks especially suitable for communal enjoyment.

❧ | Burgundy Punch

2 fifths dry red Burgundy
½ pint port
½ pint cherry brandy
Juice of 6 oranges
Juice of 3 lemons or 6 limes
2 tbsp. sugar syrup to taste
Lemon and orange peel
2 quarts club soda

Mix all ingredients, except fruit peels and club soda, in a large punch bowl with a cake of ice. Garnish with slices of orange and lemon peel. Just before serving, add club soda and stir in gently. SERVES ABOUT 30.

The *Sangaree* began its existence as a gentle, refreshing wine drink in great favor with the ladies of another age, who were unaccustomed to atomic aperitifs. Its name comes from *Sangri*, a drink of Portuguese origins, and it is basically wine, sweetened and served with or without ice in a tumbler with a pinch of nutmeg. Today's Sangarees are made with anything alcoholic, including all manner of spirits, hard cider, and even beer and ale.

❧ | Port Sangaree

1 tsp. sugar to taste
4–6 oz. port
Freshly grated nutmeg

Place several ice cubes in a 10-oz. glass; add sugar and wine; stir well until sugar is dissolved; grate nutmeg on top.

Krambambuli Punch is an old-time Swiss invention that we discovered on a cold winter's eve in the lovely old city of Lausanne overlooking Lake Geneva. The addition of arak and dark Jamaica rum makes this an ideal *après-ski* potion.

🍂 | Krambambuli Punch

2 fifths dry red wine
2 oranges
2 lemons
1 cup sugar
1 pint dark Jamaica rum
1 pint Batavia arak

Heat wine and pour into a preheated, flameproof punch bowl. Add juice of oranges and lemons and slices of the peel. Put sugar in a long-handled ladle and add a little rum and arak; ignite and flame until sugar is melted. Mix sugar with wine and add the remainder of the spirits. Serve in mugs.
SERVES ABOUT 20.

Possibly the most famous of all wine concoctions is the *Champagne Cocktail*. There are actually many champagne cocktail recipes, some of them dating from the Gay Nineties, when champagne was the "in" drink.

🍂 | Champagne Cocktail

1 sugar cube
Angostura Bitters
Brut champagne

Place a sugar cube in a chilled champagne saucer, saturate with bitters, and fill with very cold champagne.

Carbonated beverages, whether natural or artificially laced with carbon dioxide, have a certain zestiness that brightens even a drab, ordinary whiskey highball. Carbonated wine drinks are especially refreshing. They have a quality that the Germans refer to as *spritzig* or *spritzy*. It really needs no translation. *Spritzers* are the highballs of the wine world, and some people think that they taste better than the spiritous kind.

?◈ | *Rhine Wine Spritzer*

4 oz. Rhine wine	Mix gently in a chilled 10-oz. glass with
4 oz. club soda	several ice cubes.

In merry England around 1800, the prince regent had acquired a strong taste for a delicious but authoritative potion made of the following: three bottles of champagne, two bottles of Madeira, one bottle of hock (Rhine wine), one bottle of orange curaçao, one bottle of brandy, one pint of rum, two bottles of soda water "flavored with 4 pounds of bloom raisins, Seville oranges, lemons, and white candy-sugar diluted with green tea." This infusion became known as *Regent's Punch*. The following is a simplified recipe that can be made in a bowl or as an individual drink. The cold version of this punch is given in chapter III.

?◈ | *Regent's Punch #1*

1 tsp. honey to taste	Spoon honey into a large preheated mug
Hot tea	and dissolve with a little hot tea. Add
4 oz. sauterne	warmed sauterne, Madeira, and rum.
2 oz. Madeira	Mix well, fill up with additional hot tea,
1 oz. dark Jamaica rum	and top off with a dash of curaçao.
Curaçao	

The *Vermouth Cassis* has been with us for quite some time and remains to this day a classic example of what a good wine drink should be. It is also called *Export-Cassis* and *Pompier*, and although proportions may vary, it is nevertheless simply a delightful blending of dry vermouth and crème de cassis.

 | ## Vermouth Cassis

2–3 oz. dry vermouth
1 oz. crème de cassis
Club soda

Mix vermouth and cassis in a chilled 10-oz. glass with ice cubes and fill with club soda.

A variation of Vermouth Cassis is *Vin Blanc Cassis*, now called *Kir*, named after the late Canon Felix Kir, the popular and picturesque mayor of Dijon, who died in 1968 at the age of ninety-two. This bright, mild wine mixture is made without ice or soda.

Kir

3½ oz. dry white wine
½ oz. crème de cassis

Mix well-chilled white wine and cassis in a large balloon-shaped wineglass.

The *Americano*, which has quickly become a modern-day classic wine drink, is Italy's answer to the French Vermouth Cassis. It is made with Campari, a bitter aperitif, which, because of its high alcoholic content (48 proof), does not technically qualify as a true wine. In any case, the Americano is truly a wine drink of distinction, inasmuch as sweet vermouth is an essential and major ingredient.

❧ | Americano

1½ oz. Campari
1½ oz. sweet vermouth
Club soda
Lemon or orange peel

Stir Campari and vermouth with ice and pour into a tumbler with one or two ice cubes and a little club soda. Twist lemon or orange peel over drink and drop into glass.

The popularity of the *Dubonnet Cocktail* is richly deserved, for it has all the attributes of both a good cocktail and a marvelous wine drink. The original recipe specifies gin, but vodka may be substituted if desired.

❧ | Dubonnet Cocktail

1½ oz. gin
1½ oz. Dubonnet
Lemon peel

Stir gin and Dubonnet with ice; strain and serve in a chilled cocktail glass. Twist lemon peel over drink and drop into glass.

The *Bamboo Cocktail* is another all-time classic. It is also known as the *Amour Cocktail*; some recipes call for sweet vermouth, but dry vermouth seems more in keeping with modern tastes.

❧ | Bamboo Cocktail

1½ oz. dry sherry
1½ oz. dry vermouth
Dash of Angostura Bitters

Stir all ingredients well with ice; strain and serve in a chilled cocktail glass.

The following recipe was a favorite at the bar in the old Waldorf-Astoria. If nothing else, it surely bears the most poetic name ever devised for a mixed drink.

₰ | *Whispers of the Frost*

1 oz. rye or bourbon whiskey
1 oz. dry sherry
1 oz. port
Sugar to taste
Lemon peel (optional)

Stir all ingredients, except garnish, with ice; strain and serve in a chilled cocktail glass. Add a twist of lemon peel if you wish.

There is an axiom in the drink-mixing business to the effect that there is really no such thing as a completely new drink, just variations on old, old themes. Even so, seemingly minor innovations on basic formulations can produce striking changes in the taste of a drink. Some of these variations are masterful and through the use of subtle accents produce just the right blending of flavors. When this happens, the result is a drink that may one day qualify as a classic through popular acceptance and its ability to weather the vicissitudes of time and fashion.

Wine drinks require special care, for in many cases the flavors involved are delicate, subtle, and fleeting. There are also many kinds and degrees of taste sensations within a single wine category such as sherry, which ranges from very sweet to very dry. Recipes for wine drinks are particularly subject to adjustment by the mixer because of the many changes that may affect the taste of a wine from year to year even though it is pressed from grapes from the same vineyard and processed by the same vintner. Thus, not even the classic wine drinks listed here should be considered inviolate as far as proportions are concerned.

Tastes in drinks change just as surely as dress styles go in and out of vogue; trends in what people like to drink can be charted as precisely as trends in social attitudes, politics, or the price of beefsteak. In recent years there has been a steady, inexorable swing away from sweetness, often equated with "heaviness," in drinks to dryness, which is characterized as "lightness." Personal preference is, as with all food and drink recipes, the final arbiter. We have witnessed the progress of the martini from half gin and half dry vermouth, popular in the twenties, to the present-day version, which contains only the faintest traces of vermouth. In the era when it was spawned as New York's answer to the martini (a San Francisco invention?), the Manhattan could properly be considered a wine drink, since sweet vermouth comprised at least half of its content. But, alas, the trend to dryness has gradually removed it, along with many other concoctions that graced the pages of drink books compiled before World War II, from the wine drink category.

If many of the classic and near-classic drink recipes in this chapter seem to be rather sweet, it is because the very nature of true wine drinks prohibits them from ever attaining the dryness of a twenty-to-one martini. However, wine drinks will more than make up in flavor, satisfaction, and staying power what they may lack in alcoholic content. And unlike many drinks consisting exclusively of strong spirits, wine formulations offer the inventive mixologist with opportunity for creative exercises limited only by his patience, ingenuity, and the size of his bank account.

Some of the recipes that follow are recent innovations, but most have been around for a long time and have maintained their popularity. All were selected because they are highly drinkable—a solid test for any drink formula—and because, in my humble opinion, they exemplify those qualities that result in the kind of drink a wine lover would love to drink.

 | *Sanctuary*

2 oz. Dubonnet
1 oz. Amer Picon
1 oz. Cointreau
Lemon peel

Stir liquid ingredients with ice and serve in a chilled cocktail glass with a twist of lemon peel.

This drink was prepared by the Savoy Hotel's famed bartender, Harry Craddock, in honor of Princess Mary's wedding celebration on February 28, 1922.

ಎ | *Princess Mary's Pride*

2 oz. calvados or apple brandy
1 oz. Dubonnet
1 oz. dry vermouth
Lemon peel

Stir calvados, Dubonnet, and vermouth with ice and serve in a chilled cocktail glass with a twist of lemon peel.

If you omit the dry vermouth and use equal parts of Dubonnet and calvados, you will have a *Bentley*, another product of the Roaring Twenties, named, presumably, not for a princess but for an equally regal automobile (see chapter IV).

* * *

I chanced upon this champagne concoction in an elegant hotel overlooking the sea in Durban, South Africa. It bears the improbable name *Virgin's Prayer*, the origin of which is obscure. I can't imagine anyone remaining a virgin for very long after drinking a couple of these.

ಎ | *Virgin's Prayer*

1 oz. gin
½ oz. Cointreau
Dash dry sherry
Champagne

Chill gin, Cointreau, and sherry and pour in a tall champagne tulip; fill to the brim with cold champagne.

According to legend, this drink was a great favorite of Ernest Hemingway. It was named for one of his many distinguished literary works.

𑄳 | *Death in the Afternoon*

1½ oz. Pernod
Brut champagne

Chill Pernod by mixing quickly with several ice cubes in a tumbler; strain into a chilled champagne glass and fill with cold brut champagne.

The *Tempter* and *Tinton* cocktails are old-time drinks, born before World War I.

𑄳 | *Tempter Cocktail*

2 oz. port
2 oz. apricot brandy

Stir and serve in a chilled cocktail glass.

𑄳 | *Tinton Cocktail*

2 oz. port
2 oz. applejack

Stir and serve in a chilled cocktail glass.

If you add orange juice to the Tinton recipe, you have a drink called *The Philadelphian*. (See chapter VI.)

*   *   *

There are several recipes for the *Wedding Belle*. This is a favorite version.

ઠ | *Wedding Belle*

1½ oz. gin
1½ oz. Dubonnet
½ oz. cherry brandy
½ oz. orange juice

Shake with ice and serve in a chilled cocktail glass.

A variation on the above, omitting the gin, is called:

ઠ | *The Dubonnet Fizz*

3 oz. Dubonnet
1 tsp. cherry brandy
Juice of half an orange
Juice of half a lemon
Champagne or club soda

Shake Dubonnet, brandy, and fruit juices with ice and strain into a tall Collins glass. Fill with champagne or club soda.

Reputedly, this formidable concoction was the invention and favorite libation of Richard William Clark, the famous Old West figure immortalized in the *Deadwood Dick* novels of E. L. Wheeler.

ઠ | *The Yellow Daisy Cocktail*

1½ oz. gin
1½ oz. dry vermouth
¾ oz. cherry brandy
¾ oz. Grand Marnier
Dash of Pernod

Mix all ingredients and shake with ice; serve in a chilled Delmonico or whiskey sour glass.

Champagne is one of the most versatile of all drink-making ingredients, and some devotees of the bubbly have suggested that it be substituted wherever possible in place of soda in the blending of drinks. Many, many champagne drinks have been enjoyed through the years; here are some outstanding representative examples of good champagne mixtures.

ᕙ | *Champagne Cup*

2 tbsp. sugar syrup or to
    taste
4 oz. cognac
2 oz. curaçao
1 oz. Grand Marnier
Orange and pineapple
    slices
Maraschino cherries
Mint sprigs
2 fifths Brut champagne

Mix all ingredients, except champagne, with ice and stir well. Just before serving, gently mix in champagne.
SERVES 10.

France's celebrated rail line may have given its name to this concoction.

ᕙ | *The Blue Train Special*

2 oz. cognac
2 oz. pineapple syrup or
    sweetened pineapple
    juice
Brut champagne

Mix cognac and syrup with ice and pour into a 10-oz. Collins glass; add more cracked ice if necessary. Fill to the brim with crackling cold champagne.

🐌 Morning Glory

½ oz. Cointreau
½ oz. cherry brandy
Dash of Angostura Bitters
Brut champagne
Orange peel

Mix Cointreau, brandy, and bitters with ice in a 10-oz. Collins glass and fill to the top with champagne. Garnish with orange peel.

Punch recipes abound, but this fine old recipe is very hard to match:

🐌 Bombay Punch

1 fifth cognac
1 fifth dry sherry
1 pint curaçao
4 oz. maraschino liqueur
Orange and lemon slices
Maraschino cherries
4 fifths Brut champagne

Mix all liquid ingredients, except champagne and garnishes, in a large punch bowl containing a block of ice. Let stand for an hour before serving so flavors can mingle. Garnish with orange and lemon slices and maraschino cherries. Gently stir in champagne just before serving. Makes approximately 30 drinks.

Vermouth in its many forms is, without any doubt, the most ubiquitous of the great company of alcoholic beverages available for pleasurable consumption. In a later chapter, we will devote considerable space to the exploration of the many drink combinations made possible by these aromatized wines. In the meantime, here are some reliable recipes that have classic qualities.

æ | *The Weesuer Special Cocktail*

¾ oz. dry vermouth
¾ oz. sweet vermouth
¾ oz. curaçao
¾ oz. gin
½ tsp. Pernod

Mix all ingredients; stir with ice, and strain into a chilled cocktail glass.

The introduction of brandy in place of gin and just a dollop of curaçao yields a slightly different drink with a slightly intimidating name:

æ | *The Whip*

¾ oz. dry vermouth
¾ oz. sweet vermouth
1½ oz. brandy
½ tsp. curaçao
Dash of Pernod

Stir spirits with ice and strain into a chilled cocktail glass.

Undoubtedly one of the earliest vermouth cocktails was a mixture of sweet and dry. The *Addington* is an old standard.

æ | *Addington*

1½ oz. dry vermouth
1½ oz. sweet vermouth
Club soda
Orange peel

Mix vermouths with ice and pour into a tall Collins glass with ice cubes. Fill with club soda and twist an orange peel over the top.

A short version of this drink can be made by omitting the club soda. Mix the vermouths with ice and a dash of orange bitters and strain into a cocktail glass.

*　　*　　*

Judging by the number of drink recipes containing both, sherry and vermouth are a compatible pair. The popular recipes usually are known by many different names. A case in point:

ಶ | Reform Cocktail

1½ oz. dry sherry ¾ oz. sweet vermouth Dash of orange bitters	Mix with ice and strain into a chilled cocktail glass.

This cocktail was named after a venerable London club. The *Adonis Cocktail* is made exactly the same way, intended, apparently, for use by nonmembers. When equal parts of sherry and sweet vermouth are used with a dash of orange bitters, it is known as an *East Indian Cocktail*. When the Angostura Bitters are substituted in place of orange bitters and several dashes of Pernod are added, this mixture is called a *Brazil Cocktail*.

If you hanker for something stronger, try a

ಶ | Bombay Cocktail

1½ oz. brandy ¾ oz. dry vermouth ¾ oz. sweet vermouth 2 dashes of curaçao	Mix with ice and strain into a chilled cocktail glass.

There are many versions of the Bombay Cocktail (see Chapter IV), just as there are varieties of other brandy-vermouth concoctions with mysterious names such as *Diabolo*.

🎜 | *Diabolo #1*

1½ oz. brandy
1½ oz. dry vermouth
2 dashes of orange bitters
Dash of Angostura Bitters
Lemon peel

Mix all ingredients, except lemon peel, with ice and strain into a chilled cocktail glass. Twist lemon peel over the top.

🎜 | *Diabolo #2*

1½ oz. white port
1 oz. dry vermouth
Several dashes of lemon
   juice
Lemon peel

Shake all ingredients, except garnish, with ice and strain into a chilled cocktail glass. Serve with a twist of lemon peel.

A number of classic wine drinks use port as a base. One recipe utilizing white port is *The Broken Spur Cocktail*.

🎜 | *The Broken Spur Cocktail*

1½ oz. white port
¾ oz. gin
¾ oz. sweet vermouth
1 egg yolk
½ tsp. anisette
Freshly grated nutmeg

Mix all ingredients, except nutmeg, with ice in a blender; serve in a chilled cocktail glass with a little nutmeg, freshly grated.

Another highly respected old port-and-egg mixture is the *Sevilla*.

ࣄ | *Sevilla*

1½ oz. light rum	Mix all ingredients, except nutmeg,
1½ oz. port	with ice in a blender; serve in a chilled
1 egg	cocktail glass with a pinch of nutmeg,
½ tsp. powdered sugar	freshly grated.
Freshly grated nutmeg	

Many clubs have their own drinks. If the Benevolent and Protective Order of Elks originated this famous old port recipe, they certainly show good taste.

ࣄ | *Elk's Own Cocktail*

1½ oz. rye or bourbon	Mix all ingredients, except nutmeg, in a
1½ oz. port	blender; serve in a chilled cocktail glass
1 egg white	with a pinch of nutmeg, freshly grated.
Juice of half a lemon	
1 tsp. sugar	
Freshly grated nutmeg	

If you serve this drink in a Collins glass with cracked ice, filled with club soda, and garnished with a slice of pineapple, it becomes a *Japanese Fizz*.

*   *   *

A milk punch can be made with gin, rum, whiskey, brandy, vodka, and a number of wines, preferably the fortified, such as sherry, port, and Madeira. The choice of port makes for a very satisfying nightcap.

🐚 | Port Milk Punch

3 oz. port
1 tsp. sugar
1 cup milk
Freshly grated nutmeg

Mix all ingredients, except nutmeg, with ice in a blender; serve in a 12-oz. Collins glass. Grate a little nutmeg over the top.

A very nourishing variation, using sherry, is a:

🐚 | Sherry Eggnog

3 oz. sherry
1 cup milk
1 egg
1 tsp. sugar or to taste
Freshly grated nutmeg

Mix all ingredients, except nutmeg, with ice in a blender; serve in a 12-oz. Collins glass with a little grated nutmeg over the top.

Another delightful eggnog recipe employs hard cider as the principal ingredient. While not properly a wine, a cider of quality can provide the base for many excellent mixed drinks. This particular formulation was a great favorite of William Henry Harrison, military hero of the battle of Tippecanoe and ninth president of the United States.

🐚 | General Harrison's Eggnog

1 cup hard cider
1 egg
Sugar syrup to taste

Mix all ingredients with ice in a blender and serve in a large chilled Collins glass.

This recipe took third place in the Belgian Drink Contest held in Brussels in 1962.

🐌 | *Alfonso Cocktail*

1½ oz. Dubonnet
½ tsp. sugar syrup to taste
Several dashes of orange or
   Angostura Bitters
Brut champagne
Lemon or orange peel
   (optional)

Mix all ingredients, except champagne and garnish, with ice; strain into a large chilled wine goblet and fill with cold champagne. Add a twist of lemon or orange peel if you wish.

A more recent innovation featuring both Dubonnet and dry vermouth is:

🐌 | *La Camargue*

¾ oz. gold label rum
¾ oz. Cointreau
¾ oz. Dubonnet
¾ oz. dry vermouth
Dash of Pernod
Lemon peel

Shake all ingredients, except garnish, with ice and serve in a chilled cocktail glass with a twist of lemon peel.

This popular old favorite summons forth nostalgic visions of a gracious but long-gone era.

ॐ | *Phoebe Snow Cocktail*

1½ oz. cognac
1½ oz. Dubonnet
Dash of Pernod

Stir all ingredients with ice and strain into a chilled cocktail glass.

Dubonnet and other excellent aperitif wines—Byrrh, St. Raphael, and Lillet, to name but a few—make superior wine drinks. Here are several very good recipes featuring aperitifs, including the following cheering cup, which is a variation of the Phoebe Snow Cocktail.

ॐ | *Weep No More*

1½ oz. cognac
1½ oz. Dubonnet
1½ oz. lime juice
Dash of maraschino liqueur

Shake all ingredients with ice and strain into a chilled cocktail glass.

A recurrent theme throughout this book is the proposition that somewhere between the never-never land of plain soda-water or white wine aperitifs and the powerhouse potations of the 1920s and 30s lies a middleground of satisfying and imaginative mixed drinks that fulfill the primary objective of the cocktail hour: relaxation with refreshments designed to give a lift to the spirit without obliterating the evening that follows.

Recognizing the needs of a growing health-and-fitness-oriented generation, the Heublein people recently decided to launch a new family of wine drinks incorporating Smirnoff vodka as an enhancer rather than the primary ingredient. Because of the modest (½ ounce) amount of spirits used, they called this new wave of aperitifs "Smirnoff Splash Collection." It was my great pleasure to develop these new drink recipes, and I am proud to present six of them here. I believe they epitomize the basic idea behind the Smirnoff Splash: using Smirnoff to add zest and emphasis to the essential flavors of wine-based drinks without going beyond the bounds of a light, moderate refreshment.

The *Kirnoff* is a new twist on the old reliable Kir:

 ## Kirnoff

3½ oz. dry white wine
Splash of Smirnoff vodka
  (½ oz.)
½ oz. creme de cassis
Lemon peel

Mix ice cold ingredients in a chilled goblet. Twist lemon peel over drink and drop into glass.

 ## Sunsplash

3 oz. dry red wine
Splash of Smirnoff vodka
  (½ oz.)
Several dashes orange
  curaçao

Stir all ingredients with ice; strain and pour into a chilled wine glass.

The *Gilbert & Sullivan* is for operetta lovers and everyone else who enjoys sherry with a little extra zip.

🎩 | Gilbert & Sullivan

3 oz. Harvey's Bristol
  Cream
Splash of Smirnoff vodka
  (½ oz.)
2–3 dashes Angostura
  Bitters

Mix all ingredients with ice in a chilled highball glass.

🎩 | Tovarich

1 oz. sweet vermouth
1 oz. Campari
Splash of Smirnoff vodka
  (½ oz.)
Club soda
Orange slice

Mix all ingredients, except club soda and orange slice, with ice cubes in a double old-fashioned glass. Add soda, stir gently, and garnish with orange slice.

🎩 | Moscow Mimosa

3 oz. brut champagne
3 oz. orange juice
Splash of Smirnoff vodka
  (½ oz.)

Gently mix all ingredients in a chilled wine glass.

This is a subtle, flavorful drink. Kirsch, framboise, or fraise work equally well in place of mirabelle or pear brandy.

❧ | *Regatta*

4 oz. brut champagne
Splash of Smirnoff vodka
Several dashes of mirabelle
   or pear brandy

Gently stir ice cold ingredients in a chilled goblet or wine glass.

Table wines, both red and white, offer many opportunities for delectable mixed drinks once you look at wines as something that can be enjoyed at any time of the day, rather than just with meals. Champagne has been acclaimed over the years as a most versatile libation, suitable for any hour of the day, and in the Mosel region of Germany it is not uncommon to see wine drunk in the morning. I can attest that a chilled *Bernkasteler* riesling taken with breakfast can make the break of day a thing of joy and beauty.

As we have seen, the practice of mixing various herbs, spices, fruit and vegetable extracts, sweeteners, and other flavorings with wine is an ancient tradition. Sangría, which has become popular in the United States in recent years, has been popular in Spain, Portugal, France, and Italy, in various forms and many recipes, for perhaps a thousand years. Needless to say, we don't use a fine *Vosne Romanée* or a *Chateau Margaux* to mix with oranges and lemons, nor do we a spritzer from a *Chateau d'Yquem* make. By the same token, the champagne called for in the foregoing recipes should not be a vintage *Dom Perignon*. There is readily available a vast variety of acceptable but undistinguished wines, both still and sparkling, that can fulfill a beneficial function—perhaps even be glorified—as a key ingredient in an expertly made wine drink.

*   *   *

The following are well-planned formulations utilizing table wines.

ટ્ | *Peach Cup*

2 fresh peaches
1 fifth dry Moselle
Powdered sugar to taste
4 oz. peach brandy
1 fifth sparkling Moselle
Maraschino cherry and
    sprig of mint (optional)

Peel and slice peaches in a bowl; add chilled dry Moselle; cover and refrigerate for 4 hours. Then add sugar to taste and peach brandy; keep cold for another hour. Just before serving, gently stir in chilled sparkling Moselle. Ladle into glasses or cups garnished with a maraschino cherry and a sprig of mint. SERVES 8 TO 10.

A more contemporary recipe, but with definite nostalgic overtones, is

ટ્ | *Waltzing Matilda*

1½ oz. passion fruit nectar
1½ oz. gin
3 oz. dry white wine
Several dashes of curaçao
Club soda or ginger ale
Maraschino cherry and
    orange peel (optional)

Shake nectar, gin, wine, and curaçao with ice and pour into a 12- or 14-oz. glass with additional cracked ice. Fill with club soda, or ginger ale if desired, and stir gently. Garnish with a maraschino cherry and orange peel.

This is an old drink with an unusual twist:

❧ | *The Almond Cocktail*

4 oz. gin
1 tsp. sugar syrup
6–8 peeled almonds
Peach kernel (optional)
¾ oz. kirsch
¾ oz. peach brandy
4 oz. dry vermouth
8 oz. sauterne

Warm gin, sugar syrup, and almonds in a saucepan with a crushed peach kernel; allow to cool slowly so the almond flavor will become infused into the mixture. Add kirsch, peach brandy, vermouth, and sauterne, or any other sweet white wine; shake well with ice, strain, and serve in chilled cocktail glasses with an almond.
SERVES 6.

No catalog of classic and near-classic concoctions would be complete without this old cold-weather bracer.

❧ | *Hot Benefactor*

1 tsp. sugar or to taste
2 oz. dry burgundy
2 oz. Jamaica rum
Lemon slice
Freshly grated nutmeg

Dissolve sugar in a saucepan with several ounces of hot water; add burgundy and rum. Quickly bring to the boiling point, but don't boil. Serve in a preheated mug with a thin slice of lemon and freshly grated nutmeg.

There are many other "benefactors," hot and cold, in the pages that follow. Some of them may be, or will become, your special favorites. These then become classics or, at the very least, standards for you in a very real sense. It is hoped that you will experiment and innovate, changing proportions, adding or replacing ingredients to suit the very special needs of your own palate. There is surely nothing immutable or fixed about a drink recipe. I have never seen one graven on stone—for it surely would be wasted labor. Tastes are dynamic and are constantly subject to change, for the individual as well as for the group.

Thus far we have had but a selective sampling of the vast world of wine drinks. Ahead are many delicious and satisfying horizons. So, grape lovers, let us press on. There are many good things to come.

II | EFFERVESCENT EMOLLIENTS

From the earliest days of our youth, things that fizz have a fascination for most of us. There is something marvelously refreshing about a carbonated soft drink, even if it is only a transient illusion brought about by all of those dancing little bubbles of carbon dioxide. When I was a teenager, I was not particularly enamored of wine, perhaps because it was served regularly in our house. I much preferred a crackling cold bottle of beer; it was tasty, thirst-quenching, and bubbly as well as cheap and readily available. Then, one fine day, for no special reason that I can recall, I found myself with a glass of cold champagne in my hot hand. It was one of the great taste experiences of my life, and I have been a champagne devotee ever since.

If you are a lover of champagne and the many other sparkling wines in that great company of what I choose to call effervescent emollients, you may best utilize the information that has been assembled here to the accompaniment of a thousand popping corks, if you put aside all of your opinions, prejudices, and preconceptions regarding the use of bubbly wines. Forget the lore and traditions of champagne, beginning with that wily old monk, Dom Perignon, who is credited with devising the means of getting the bubbles in the wine and keeping them there; forget, for the moment, that champagne is deservedly the royalty of fine wine, universal in its appeal, appropriate at any time of the day and for any reason, proper and well suited to almost any meal, a balm to the spirit and a boon to the body, always festive, refreshing, and satisfying. Dwell not upon great vintage years and *tête de cuvées*. These should be reserved for treasured moments in the precincts of *haute cuisine* to be savored in their pristine state.

Think instead as an innovative wine lover who enjoys favorite potations in a variety of forms. Think of champagne as an essential universal mixer to be blended with other spirits, flavoring agents, spices, herbs, sweeteners, and diverse constituents that yield complex and tantalizing taste experiences. The time is at hand, for never has a greater selection of sparkling, champagne-type wines of good character and quality been available in the United States at very affordable prices than now. This means that the creative mixologist has at hand a great selection of sparkling wines from Spain, France, Germany, Italy, and the United States, and while they are not, strictly speaking, champagnes (this is a term that should be reserved for those wines produced in the well-defined Champagne district, which lies about ninety miles northeast of Paris), they are, nevertheless, made by the very same *méthode champenoise* that is used to produce genuine champagne. The Spanish vintners are turning out superb sparkling wines at unbeatable prices. My personal choice from a number of very drinkable products are Gran Codorniu and Codorniu Brut Clásico, which are made in Codorniu's sprawling, modern, spic-and-span wineries in San Sudurni de Noya near Barcelona. A French sparkling chardonnay, Brut Royal Blanc de Blancs from the Côtes du Jura, in the eastern part of France near the Swiss border, is dry, crisp, and well balanced enough to fool experts in a blind tasting. And there are many others, including several excellent American entries at prices that won't make you wince when you mix them with less noble ingredients. While specific recommendations are not critical when selecting a sparkling, champagne-type wine for use in a fruit punch or a cocktail, it should be pointed out that a substandard sparkling wine will not be improved when comingled with other flavors, nor will it contribute anything to the end result save a few bubbles and an off taste. I have attended festive occasions where vintage champagne made a memorable punch. To the purist, it was, no doubt, simply the prostitution of a noble wine, but to the affluent host, concerned only with serving the very best, it was a small price to pay for an elegant refreshment.

A selection of elegant refreshments is presented herewith for your delectation, beginning with some variations on the champagne cocktail. Whether you elect to use the real thing or a good champagne-type wine depends largely upon your taste, disposition, and the thickness of your wallet. Only time and some effort in determining the best way to satisfy the needs of your palate will provide the answer.

As any perceptive wine lover can quickly surmise, the basic champagne cocktail (see chapter I) is not a very imaginative endeavor and has been much improved over the years: Consider, for example, the addition of a wide range of tasty liqueurs and fruit brandies that produce cocktails at once zesty and refreshing.

A delightful variation on the popular Kir is the *Kir Royale*.

ॐ | *Kir Royale*

½ oz. crème de cassis Brut champagne	Mix crème de cassis and chilled champagne gently in a large balloon wineglass.

Paul Bocuse, the renowned French chef, likes his Kir with a jolt of framboise, an authoritative white brandy made of raspberries.

ॐ | *Paul Bocuse Special*

¾ oz. crème de cassis ¾ oz. framboise Brut champagne	Mix crème de cassis and framboise in a large chilled wineglass, then fill with champagne and stir gently. If you wish, you may substitute kirsch in place of framboise.

EFFERVESCENT EMOLLIENTS

Nan and Ivan Lyons, wine lovers *par excellance* and authors of *Someone Is Killing the Great Chefs of Europe* and *Champagne Blues*, are devotees of wine drinks like this one, named, appropriately enough, *Champagne Blues*.

🐚 | *Champagne Blues*

Brut champagne
Blue curaçao
Lemon twist

Fill a tulip glass with chilled champagne, pour in curaçao to taste. Add twist.

Since the discovery of the French 75 by American doughboys during WWI, cognac and champagne combinations have been popular. Here is a sampling of some of the more stellar concoctions:

🐚 | *Champagne Cooler*

1 oz. cognac
1 oz. Cointreau
Brut champagne
Fresh mint sprig or
    peppermint schnapps
    (optional)

Half-fill a double Old Fashioned glass with crushed ice. Add cognac and Cointreau and muddle furiously. Fill with champagne and garnish with mint sprig or float a scant teaspoon of peppermint schnapps on top.

🐚 | *The Royal Screwdriver*

Juice of a large orange
1 oz. cognac
Brut champagne

Pour cold orange juice into a large chilled goblet with cracked ice. Add cognac, champagne, and stir.

Cordial Médoc is a Bordeaux creation made of curaçao, crème de cacao, and cognac. It works well in this champagne concoction.

₰ | Champagne Médoc

1 oz. Cordial Médoc
½ oz. cognac
1½ oz. lemon juice
Sugar to taste
Brut champagne

Mix Cordial Médoc, cognac, and lemon juice with sugar to taste in a shaker or blender with cracked ice. Strain and pour into a large chilled balloon glass and fill with champagne.

This drink takes its name from a legendary purveyor of "Jersey Lightning"—also known as applejack.

₰ | Jersey Jack

1 oz. applejack or calvados
1 oz. cognac
½ oz. curaçao
1 tsp. lemon juice
Brut champagne

Mix applejack, cognac, curaçao, and lemon juice with cracked ice in a shaker or blender and pour into a large chilled goblet with more ice, if needed; fill with chilled champagne.

₰ | Strawberry Blonde

6 fresh strawberries
¾ oz. cognac
¾ oz. strawberry liqueur
Several dashes of lemon
  juice
Brut champagne

Mix all ingredients, except champagne, in a shaker or blender with cracked ice. Pour into a large chilled goblet, fill with champagne, and stir gently.

A crusta is a drink that calls for a glass lined with citrus fruit peel.

𝒆𝓵 | Cossack Crusta

1 orange
1 oz. cognac
½ oz. kümmel
1 tsp. lemon juice
Sugar to taste
Orange bitters
Brut champagne

Remove the peel from an orange in one continuous spiral and use it to line the inside of a large, chilled goblet. Mix cognac, kümmel, lemon juice, and sugar with cracked ice in a shaker or blender and pour into the goblet. Add a bit more ice, sprinkle with bitters and fill with chilled champagne.

𝒆𝓵 | Prince of Wales

¾ oz. cognac
¾ oz. Madeira
½ oz. curaçao
Dash of Angostura Bitters
Brut champagne
Orange slice

Mix all ingredients, except champagne and orange slice, in a shaker or blender with cracked ice; pour into large chilled balloon glass. Fill with cold champagne. Garnish with orange slice.

The coloring of this concoction gives it its name.

𝒆𝓵 | Champagne Canarie

1 oz. cognac
Brut champagne
Yellow Chartreuse

Pour cognac into a large chilled tulip glass, fill with cold champagne, and stir gently. Float a little yellow Chartreuse on top.

❧ | *Apricot Ambrosia*

3–4 oz. fresh apricot puree
Lemon juice
Cognac
Dash of triple sec
Apricot-flavored brandy
   (optional)
Brut champagne

Puree ripe apricots with a sieve, chinois, or mortar and pestle; sprinkle with a little lemon juice and allow to soak in a jigger of cognac in a covered dish for a few hours. Pour into a large chilled goblet, add a dash of triple sec, a dash of apricot-flavored brandy, and some cracked ice. Fill with chilled champagne.

"La Chaufrette" is, literally, a footwarmer, but this cooler will warm you up all over.

❧ | *La Chaufrette*

1 oz. cognac
½ oz. sweet vermouth
Brut champagne
Orange peel

Mix cognac and vermouth (you may use dry vermouth, if you wish) with cracked ice in a large chilled balloon glass; fill with cold champagne. Twist orange peel over glass and drop in.

And now here are some "house specials," which are always interesting and inevitably good, since the honor and reputation of a distinguished restaurant, hotel proprietor, or chef de cuisine hangs in the balance. A good place to begin might be with our own country-house champagne favorite.

EFFERVESCENT EMOLLIENTS

ॐ Trollhagen Special

1 oz. B&B liqueur
Brut champagne
Orange peel

Pour B&B into a large chilled balloon glass half-filled with cracked ice; fill with cold champagne. Twist orange peel over drink and drop in.

Fouquet's venerable restaurant on the corner of the Champs Elysée and Avenue George V, in the fashionable *8ᵉ arrondissement* in Paris, has always been a favorite rendezvous due to its convenient location and proximity to such elegant hostelries as the George V and the Prince de Galles. For those in need of a restorative after a late night, Fouquet's offers this pick-me-up potation, which is also a smashing brunch drink.

ॐ Fouquet's Pick-Me-Up

1 oz. Grand Marnier
½ oz. kirsch
2 oz. orange juice
  (optional)
Brut champagne
Orange slice

Pour Grand Marnier and kirsch into a chilled champagne glass of generous proportions. Add orange juice and a little cracked ice, if you wish, and fill with cold champagne. Garnish with orange slice.

The famed Savoy Hotel in London has long been a wellspring of original drink recipes created over the years for such signal occasions as royal weddings and coronations—and often for no occasion at all. When astronauts landed on the moon, the Savoy accorded the event proper recognition by creating a new drink named, appropriately enough, the *Moon Walk Cocktail*.

 Moon Walk Cocktail

1 oz. grapefruit juice
1 oz. Grand Marnier
Generous dash of rosewater
Brut champagne

Mix grapefruit juice, Grand Marnier, and rosewater with a little shaved ice in a large chilled stem glass; fill with cold champagne.

Harry's Bar in Venice is famous for many things: its ambience, its interesting and often famous clientele, and its generous and imaginative drinks. The fruit mixtures are well known and quite popular, and the *Bellini* is a representative example of the quality of the house.

 Bellini

3 oz. pureed peaches
Lemon juice
Maraschino liqueur
Brut champagne

Puree ripe peaches by forcing them through a sieve or chinois; sprinkle with a little lemon juice and sweeten with maraschino. Pour puree into a large chilled goblet, fill with cold champagne, and stir gently.

This is a version of another famous Harry's Bar creation, utilizing the zest and snap of pear brandy.

૨૭. | *Tintoretto*

2 oz. pureed pears
1 oz. pear brandy
Brut champagne
Fresh mint (optional)

Puree a ripe pear using a sieve or chinois and place puree in a large chilled goblet with brandy; add champagne, cracked ice, and mint.

Windows on the World, the remarkable *grande luxe* restaurant complex in the sky that offers the most spectacular views at table you will find anywhere in New York City, also excels in concocting unusual, innovative food and drink recipes. The *Poinsettia* is one of them.

૨૭. | *Poinsettia*

3 oz. cranberry juice
½ oz. Cointreau or triple
sec
3 oz. Brut champagne

Chill all ingredients well, including a large champagne glass. Mix cranberry juice and Cointreau in glass, and fill with cold champagne.

To commemorate the opening of the Waldorf-Astoria's Cocktail Terrace, where thirsts may be slaked amid refurbished Art Deco splendor, a new house drink was introduced and named in honor of this famous hotel's first restaurant director.

૨૭. | *The René Black*

½ oz. Amer Picon
Brut champagne

Pour Amer Picon into a tulip glass that has been well chilled and fill with ice-cold champagne.

The Hotel de la Poste in Cortina, Italy, is a social crossroads for skiers and other assorted holiday-seekers. Among other things, the hotel whips up such zesty and satisfying champagne drinks as the *Puccini*, a tangy combination of freshly squeezed tangerine juice and champagne. And then there is the *Pizzetti*.

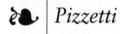 | *Pizzetti*

1 oz. cognac	Mix all ingredients except champagne
2 oz. orange juice	in a blender with cracked ice; strain and
2 oz. grapefruit juice	pour into a large chilled goblet; fill with
Brut champagne	cold champagne.

Trader Vic (Victor Bergeron) is justly famous for his many delicious and innovative rum drinks, but he strays off the plantation now and then and comes up with fine recipes *sans* rum. This is one of them, and it works—despite my feeling that anyone who makes a habit of mixing champagne and gin is looking for trouble.

In case you're wondering what "opu" means, it's the Hawaiian word for belly, according to Trader Vic.

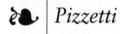 | *The Colonel's Big Opu*

Half a lime	Squeeze lime into a large chilled goblet
1 oz. gin	with cracked ice; add gin and Coin-
1 oz. Cointreau	treau; stir well and fill glass with chilled
Champagne	champagne.

Another Trader Vic invention utilizes Southern Comfort, which marries well with champagne. The only drawback is that to make this drink you must freeze some whole canned apricots in advance. Trader

Vic suggests putting them into your ice tray, one to each little compartment—which means you are either going to serve these at a party or be drinking a lot of apricots and champagne.

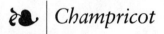 Trader Vic's Champagne-Apricot

1 frozen apricot
1 oz. Southern Comfort
Champagne

Place apricot in a chilled champagne glass with a little shaved ice; add Southern Comfort and fill glass with chilled champagne.

Another, simpler champagne-apricot cocktail is featured at the Kahala Hilton in Honolulu:

Champricot

1 fresh apricot
Champagne

Pierce apricot in several places with a fork and place in a chilled tulip glass. Fill with cold champagne. Bubbles will cause apricot to dance in the glass.

From the lovely old Hotel Queen Elizabeth in Montreal comes another interesting apricot-based house cocktail.

Le Classique

1 small canned apricot
Cognac
¾ oz. apricot-flavored
brandy
Brut champagne

Soak apricot overnight in cognac in a covered dish. Place apricot in a chilled champagne flute (if apricot is too large, slice in half); pour in about ¾ oz. apricot brandy and fill with ice-cold champagne.

The sleek, modern Vienna Hilton features an impressive variety of house drinks, many of which utilize sparkling wines called "sekt." Here is one of the more offbeat concoctions.

❧ Chemin de Fer

¾ oz. Benedictine
½ oz. scotch
½ oz. sweet vermouth
Several dashes of
  Angostura Bitters
Brut champagne

Mix all ingredients, except champagne, in a blender with cracked ice; strain and pour into a chilled tulip glass. Fill with cold champagne. Stir gently.

From the famous Ritz bar in Paris, home of the Mimosa and other fine drinks, comes this classic pick-me-up.

❧ Ritz Special Pick-Me-Up

¾ oz. cognac
¾ oz. Cointreau
4 oz. orange juice
Brut champagne

Mix all ingredients, except champagne, with lots of cracked ice in a blender and pour into a chilled balloon glass. Fill with cold champagne and stir gently.

A favorite house drink from New York's palace of *haute cuisine*, La Caravelle, is the popular *Número Uno*.

❧ Número Uno

Juice of half a lime
1 oz. vodka
Sugar to taste
Brut champagne
Fresh mint leaves, crushed

Mix lime juice, vodka, and sugar with cracked ice in a blender; strain and pour into a large chilled tulip glass. Fill with chilled champagne and garnish with mint leaves.

         EFFERVESCENT EMOLLIENTS

Paul Kovi, one of the owners of The Four Seasons, one of New York's most elegant eating places, delights in a refresher made of icy champagne with a dash of Campari. The addition of gin to champagne and Campari produces a stronger drink called the *Laguna Sport*.

🕊 | *Laguna Sport*

Champagne
¾ oz. Campari
Gin

Nearly fill a large chilled tulip glass with cold champagne. Gently stir in Campari and add a small amount of shaved ice if you wish. Float a teaspoon or more of gin on top.

This flavorful refresher, called *El Castillo Morro Bebida Fria* in Spanish, was invented especially for a presentation of new food and beverage recipes using rum; the occasion was sponsored by the Rums of Puerto Rico and held at New York's newest riverside restaurant, The Water Club, on June 15, 1983.

🕊 | *The Morro Castle Cooler*

1 oz. white Puerto Rican rum
¾ oz. triple sec or any orange liqueur
3 oz. orange juice
3 oz. champagne

Mix rum, triple sec, and orange juice in a tall Collins glass with cracked ice; gently stir in ice-cold champagne.

Champagne was made to accommodate and provide a proper counterpoint to almost any flavor. For this reason it is one of the few wines that can be drunk throughout the course of an entire banquet, beginning with the appetizer and ending with dessert. It is especially compatible with fruits and fruit flavors in the form of liqueurs and brandies. There are many possibilities for imaginative cocktails using champagne and fruits. The following is a roundup of some of the more popular combinations.

ﾧ | *Champagne Fraise*

¾ oz. strawberry liqueur
Dash kirsch
Brut champagne
2–3 fresh strawberries

Swirl strawberry liqueur and kirsch around the inside of a tulip glass that has been well chilled. Fill with iced champagne and add strawberries.

ﾧ | *Champagne Mirabelle*

½ oz. eau de vie de
**   mirabelle**
Dash of triple sec
Brut champagne

Pour mirabelle into a chilled glass, add triple sec, and fill with cold champagne. Stir gently.

ﾧ | *Champagne Hawaiian*

2 oz. pineapple juice
Angostura Bitters
Champagne
Pineapple stick

Mix pineapple juice and bitters in a chilled balloon glass with a little shaved ice. Fill with cold champagne and garnish with pineapple stick.

৯ | Champagne Framboise

¼ cup fresh raspberries
½ oz. framboise
Brut champagne

Crush raspberries and push through a sieve to remove seeds. Add puree to a large chilled goblet and mix with framboise. Fill with cold champagne and stir gently.

৯ | The Apple Blossom

2 oz. apple sauce
1 oz. calvados
Sugar to taste
Brut champagne

Mix all ingredients, except champagne, in a blender with cracked ice; pour into a large chilled goblet. Fill with cold champagne and stir gently.

৯ | Champagne and Grape Juice

2 oz. white or red grape
   juice
Brut champagne

Pour grape juice with a little shaved ice into a chilled goblet. Fill with ice-cold champagne and stir gently.

The following was created for those who believe that a champagne cocktail should be more than just a sugar cube doused with a dash of bitters. Rosewater, which is made from rose petals in France and imparts a subtle, delicate flavor, is used in this drink.

🐌 | *Champagne Supreme*

½ oz. Grand Marnier
½ oz. curaçao
½ oz. maraschino liqueur
Several dashes of rosewater
Brut champagne

Mix all ingredients, except champagne, in a blender with cracked ice; pour into a large chilled goblet. Fill with cold champagne and stir gently.

Those who enjoy the subtle flavor of the French aperitif wine Lillet will find this a simple, satisfying drink.

🐌 | *Champagne Lillet*

3–4 oz. Lillet
Brut champagne
Orange peel

Pour Lillet into a chilled goblet with a little shaved ice. Fill with cold champagne, stir gently; twist orange peel over glass and drop into drink.

The last batch of champagne libations falls into the category of "oddball" drinks, which is not to say that they are not tempting and tasty, but rather that they are designed for those adventurous souls who enjoy trying new things.

🐌 | *Carlotta's Dream*

1½ oz. tequila
Juice of half a lemon or
   lime
Sugar to taste
Champagne

Mix all ingredients, except champagne, in blender with cracked ice and pour into a large chilled goblet. Fill with cold champagne and stir gently.

≈ | *Sutton Place Sundae*

Generous tbsp. vanilla ice
  cream
2–3 dashes of curaçao
2–3 dashes of cognac
2–3 dashes of kirsch
1 tsp. maraschino cherry
  syrup
Brut champagne

Chill a large (12- to 14-oz.) goblet; add ice cream and all other ingredients except champagne. Fill with cold champagne and stir very gently.

For those who hanker for the flavor of pine in their champagne, the enterprising staff of the Kahala Hilton in Honolulu has devised this unusual cocktail.

≈ | *Chamberry Cocktail*

½ oz. Chambord liqueur
Brut champagne
2–3 pine needles
Fresh raspberry (optional)

Pour Chambord into a chilled tulip glass and fill with ice-cold champagne. Twist pine needles and float on top of drink; or you may garnish with a fresh raspberry or two.

Sooner or later almost everyone who owns a syphon that carbonates water through the use of little carbon-dioxide cartridges has a go at making his own sparkling wine; some seem to be more successful than others. But there is a trick to it and that is to avoid squirting the carbonated wine out through the spout as you would if your syphon contained only charged water. You must remove the top of the syphon after carbonating wine and pour it out directly into your glass. Obviously, no matter how effectively your syphon carbonates beverages, your wine will not approach the flavor qualities and zest of sparkling wine made painstakingly by the *méthode champenoise*. If it were all that easy, everybody would be doing it and the champagne makers would fall upon difficult times. But if you are in the mood to do a little experimenting, just follow the simple directions.

Choose a white or red wine. A Chablis or a chardonnay is a good choice for white, or a light red such as an Italian Valpolicella, a California Zinfandel, or a light French Bordeaux. Pour wine into syphon to the filling level marked on the syphon bottle and proceed to carbonate the contents according to the manufacturer's instructions. Before serving, place syphon in refrigerator and chill for four to eight hours. When ready to serve, hold syphon over the sink and carefully relieve the pressure inside, then unscrew the top and pour into glasses.

If all goes well, you will have a refreshing spritzer without the dilution that would occur if you simply mixed club soda with wine. If all does not go well, relegate your syphon exclusively to the business of making seltzer water, open a bottle of real champagne, and drink a silent toast to the anonymous Parisian who said, "Champagne is the wine a young man drinks on the evening of his first mistake." Take comfort in the knowledge that what you have learned in your efforts to make sparkling wine the easy way will greatly enhance your appreciation of the real thing from this time onward.

The spritzer has been much vaunted in recent years by those concerned with caloric intake, keeping fit, and generally limiting their alcoholic intake to help keep a trim figure and a clear head. While these are admirable pursuits, the fact remains that this wine-and-soda mixture is at best a drink for sluggards with little imagination or taste for wine. If you must make wine drinks with club soda or seltzer, at least choose those combinations that will produce interesting flavors. Here are a few candidates:

੨ৱ | Wine Tonic

4 oz. dry white wine
Dash of lime juice
Several dashes of grenadine
½ oz. vodka
Tonic water or seltzer

Put some ice cubes into a large Collins glass; add wine, lime juice, grenadine, and vodka. Stir well and fill with tonic or seltzer.

❧ | Ginger Peachie

4 oz. green ginger wine
½ oz. peach-flavored
   brandy
Club soda
Lemon peel

Place some ice cubes into a large Collins glass; add wine and brandy; fill with club soda. Add twist of lemon peel and stir well.

❧ | Byrrh Highball

4 oz. Byrrh
½ oz. crème de cassis
Club soda
Lemon or orange peel

Pour Byrrh, cassis, and a few ice cubes into a large Collins glass, fill with club soda, and stir well. Add twist of lemon or orange peel.

❧ | Cassis Highball

1 oz. crème de cassis
Several dashes of kirsch
Club soda
Lemon peel

Pour cassis, kirsch, and a few ice cubes into a highball glass, fill with soda, and stir. Add twist of lemon peel.

❧ | Orange Cup

4 oz. dry white wine
4 oz. orange juice
½ oz. Cointreau
Club soda

Mix white wine, orange juice, and Cointreau in a large Collins glass with some cracked ice; fill with club soda. Stir gently.

This is a Hawaiian cooler, invented in New York for friends who were yearning to be back in Honolulu.

ਟ੍ਰ | *Honolulu Surf Rider*

4 oz. pineapple juice
Juice of half a lime
½ oz. Southern Comfort
3 oz. Chablis or sauterne
Club soda
Pineapple stick (optional)

Mix all liquid ingredients, except soda and garnish, in a blender with cracked ice. Pour into a large Collins glass and fill with soda. Stir and garnish with pineapple stick.

Wine lemonades were popular as a light drink for warm weather when Great-grandmother was young. Great-grandma or no, they are quite refreshing, and you can create endless variations.

ਟ੍ਰ | *Basic Wine Lemonade*

Juice of half a lemon
Sugar to taste
4 oz. dry or sweet wine,
    white or red
Club soda

Mix lemon juice, sugar, and wine in a large Collins glass with cracked ice; stir until sugar is dissolved and fill with club soda.

ਟ੍ਰ | *Rosy Lemonade*

Juice of half a lemon
Sugar to taste
4 oz. Mateus rosé wine
Generous dash of
    grenadine
Club soda

Mix all ingredients, except soda, in a large Collins glass with cracked ice and fill with soda. Stir gently.

🍷 Wine Collins

4 oz. port, Madeira, or Marsala
Squeeze of lime
Lemon-lime soda
Maraschino cherry

Pour wine and squeeze of lime (and peel) into a large Collins glass half-filled with cracked ice. Fill to top with lemon-lime soda; stir and garnish with cherry.

So much for spritzer-type drinks. Frankly, I feel that many of these drinks would be better off if champagne or a champagne-type wine were used in place of soda or other carbonated beverages. I enjoy soft drinks in their essential role as thirst-quenchers, but not, generally speaking, as an accompaniment to wines. But be not dismayed, spritzer lovers, there are more recipes featuring club soda in the chapter on punches and mini-punches, which have become popularized as coolers. Here again, when recipes calling for champagne *and* club soda in the punch bowl are carefully considered, my instincts tell me that some of these formulations had their origins in the Great Depression and that the use of club soda is simply a means of extending the punch and economizing on the champagne.

In the interest of more creative and authentic wine potables, the wine lover is advised to seek out and sample the many wonderful bubbly wines that are available—old favorites such as sparkling Moselle and sparkling Saumur, as well as the many high-quality champagne-type wines being produced in other parts of the Continent—and take a good look at the very fine sparkling wines being produced in California and New York State. These last categories are not to be confused with some of the older, sweet, grapey varieties that bear little resemblance to authentic champagnes and other fine, dry, well-balanced wines made by the *méthode champenoise*. A new day has dawned in American wine-growing areas, and, happily, we are producing not merely a counterfeit sparkling wine with the word *champagne* on the label but rather a unique generation of bright, vibrant wines with flavor and character found nowhere else in the world.

III | A PROLIFERATION OF PUNCHES

What could be more festive than a gathering of old friends around a punch bowl, its intricate, faceted glass reflecting the dancing flames in the fireplace, the flickering candles casting a warm glow on the laughing, happy faces surrounding a table groaning with a tantalizing array of delicacies of every description? The storm howls without; within, all is cozy and bright as cups are lifted, toasts are made, conversation grows more animated, and the room rocks with revelry. It might be a scene from *The Pickwick Papers* with a punch seen to by Samuel Weller, or the memorable dinner at Todger's, in *Martin Chuzzlewit*, climaxed by Mr. Pecksniff's fall into the fireplace. Or it could be a quiet evening with a few friends reminiscing around the community cocktail font, and sipping with relish a punch that you have made. Standing at one side, you can say with the understandable pride of Lord Pembroke to his assembled guests gathered by the flowing bowl, "There, gentlemen, is my champagne and my claret. I am no great judge (of wine) and I give you these on the authority of my wine merchant; but I can answer for my punch, for I made it myself."

Like other drinks, punches go in and out of vogue, but a truly well conceived punch, whether served in a bowl to many or in a glass to an individual, is always popular. Of course, we are talking about exemplary refreshment, not the kinds of punch we have all been subjected to at one time or another at the annual outing of the Chowder and

Marching Society or at the reception given in honor of the new Home-coming Queen. These acidic assaults on our defenseless palates are all too frequent when the basic rules of proper punch-making are circum-vented, either through ignorance or foolish economy. The latter is a matter of personal or corporate financial resources, beyond the pur-view of this discourse. One fact should be recognized, however: One bottle of brandy, vodka, or whatever and a couple of bottles of sherry or port mixed with a mélange of fruit juices and seltzer cannot stretch to accommodate a reception for a hundred people. It won't work. You will be found out. Even those unsophisticated about the lore of wines and spirits recognize the fact when they are served a thin, watery, insipid, pusillanimous mixture masquerading as a punch. If your purse strings are stretched to the breaking point, you are better off in buying a keg of draft beer. It will serve the multitude well, and it is the real thing—not a spurious imitation.

The origin of the word *punch* is reputed to come from the Hin-dustani word *pānch* meaning "five" (as in *panchāmrit*, a mixture of five substances), which alludes to "the rule of five," traditional ele-ments of a punch: one part sour, one part sweet, one part strong, one part weak, and a good measure of spices. Although there is consider-able division of opinion as to whether this is the true source of the word *punch*,* the concept of five diverse ingredients suggests that a *balance of contrasting flavors* is an important factor in punch-making, as indeed it is. But this is easier said than done, as we shall see, and not all punches have just five categories of ingredients. Some have more, some less, but the important thing is balance between whatever ingre-dients are used.

---

* Many fanciful tales abound regarding the origins of food and drink names. The many explanations for the provenance of the word *cocktail* clearly demonstrate that some etymologists missed their calling. They should have become writers of fiction. It is a tenuous bridge that connects the Hindu word *pānch* with the English word *punch*, and it may not be a bridge at all, for the drinking of punch is not a custom among either Hindus or Moslems—they are abstainers. Some authorities argue that the word *punch* was more likely a short form of *puncheon*, a cask that holds about eighty gallons of liquid such as rum. Since British sailors were served their rum rations from small casks, it seems plausable that this contraction came to mean anything spiritous that was served out of a large container. Decide for yourself.

Before covering the basics of punch construction, a word on equipment. A punch can be made in anything that doesn't leak: an oaken bucket, a stockpot, a sawed-off keg, a soup kettle, or even a hollowed-out cake of ice. But there is no real substitute for a lovely silver, crystal, or china punch bowl surrounded by cups and strategically located so it can function as a gathering place for assembled friends. If you don't have a real punch bowl, borrow one, or rent one from a caterer. Proper presentation is half the battle. Also, give a thought to table decorations. Besides the conventional holly at Christmastime and the traditional garlands for wedding receptions, there are exotic tropical blossoms and greens that can turn an ordinary table into a garden of delights to rival those created by Trader Vic at his various Polynesian-style emporiums—where, incidentally, one can find some very distinguished rum punches.

The basics of a good punch are simple, but as any martini devotee knows, simple things are not always easy. First, plan your punch to fit the occasion. A punch in springtime for a graduation celebration should be light, refreshing, and not too authoritative since a wide range of people will be represented, from the art teacher ("Well, just *one*, and please, just half a cup") to the former captain of the wrestling team ("Punch! That's for kids. Gimme a real drink"). A punch for a stag affair or a steaming bowl prepared for *après-ski* on a bitter cold night should be engineered to suit the guests and the circumstances. While this *sounds* sensible enough, I can recall a college commencement soirée where Fish House Punch was served with devastating results. As anyone who has had a serious encounter with it knows, this delicious and historic beverage packs a powerhouse punch—no pun intended—and was never designed by our nation's founders for protracted drinking bouts.

Fresh fruits are essential. Prepared cocktail mixes, both liquid and dry, have their places, especially for the making of quick and easy cocktails when fresh fruits are unavailable or unstorable—on a small boat, for example—but the ritual of the punch bowl demands the very best, and fresh fruits are the very best for punches. Squeeze them fresh and strain them well before combining with any other ingredient. Do not load up your bowl with fruit pulp, and use restraint with garnishes of fruit slices. A few are sufficient. A lot interfere with serving, and besides, your guests didn't come to your party to fill up on orange and lemon slices.

Ice cubes, while a boon to most civilized drink-making, are out for punches. They cause too much dilution, and a watery punch, no matter how well conceived, is never acceptable. Use a large cake of ice, or at the very least remove the dividers from your ice cube trays and freeze large slabs of ice to chill your punch. Chill all of your ingredients in advance. To avoid excess melting, it is important that wines and spirits be cold—after all, they comprise a large portion of the liquid content of the punch bowl. Some people enjoy freezing fruits such as cherries, grapes, and strawberries in the ice that is used for the punch bowl. Do so if you wish, but of far greater importance is the water you use to make ice. If you live in an area where the tap water is heavily chlorinated or has an unpleasant mineral taste, you will be surprised how good your drinks will taste if you make your ice cubes with bottled spring water. The same is true of your punches. Furthermore, your ice will probably be crystal clear, which in itself will add a little sparkle to your punch bowl.

It is important that champagne and other sparkling wines be withheld until the very last minute, then stirred gently into the punch mixture. The same applies to club soda, seltzer, ginger ale, and other carbonated beverages. The purpose is to conserve the effervescence as much as possible. Nothing succeeds as well as a bright, zesty punch with lots of fizz. Finally, keep a batch of punch, chilled and in reserve, in your refrigerator. Due to the high alcoholic content, it will keep for several weeks in a covered container under refrigeration. If your punch is a smash hit and your guests begin to scrape the bottom of your bowl, having a refill in reserve will save much last-minute rushing around. More important, you will avoid the grievous error of attempting to stretch the punch by adding fruit juice, seltzer, or water. The only honorable means of extending your punch is to *add more punch* to the bowl, using the very same formula you used at the outset.

The number of servings from a bowl of punch can only be approximated. If you estimate that each serving will be roughly 4 ounces (punch cups are usually smaller than an ordinary teacup), then for each quart of punch you will get about 8 servings. The *Regent's Punch* recipe below should give you approximately 84 servings. This is arrived at by adding up all the ounces of liquid, including the oranges and lemons. An orange of medium size should yield about ⅓ cup or 2½ ounces of juice. A lemon should give you 3 tablespoons or about 1½ ounces of juice. No allowance is made for ice meltage, which, in a properly chilled punch, *not* sitting in a sunny window on a scorching August afternoon, should not be a significant factor. When planning a party, caterers have a way of arriving at target estimates by adapting to the circumstances. If the party has more than an average number of heavy drinkers, the caterer, who is working against a budget, will serve lighter drinks, add more ice, use more soda or whatever. This is understandable, but not for a private social gathering. The host should be guided by only one inviolable rule: *Never place yourself in the position of having to tell your guests that you've run out of food or drink.*

And now that you have had a crash course in punch-building basics, let's see how you perform with jigger, bar spoon, and bowl.

If ever there was a perfect punch mixer, champagne is it. It adds zest, crispness, flavor; it blends well with almost any fruit, spice, or flavoring agent you can name; and it marries well with other spirits. It is a flavor catalyst. And it helps immensely in the precise business of balancing a collection of flavors with one another. This is an important attribute of every really good punch. For all of these reasons, it is not surprising that there are probably more punch recipes based upon using champagne as an essential ingredient than all the rest of the world of wines and spirits put together.

Our ancestors in England and various parts of Europe were great punch lovers and have left us a legacy of fine punch recipes that have stood the test of time. Sampling some of these historic punches seems like a good way to begin. (*Note:* A "bottle" is a standard fifth [25.4 oz.] or approximately 750 ml.)

Fit for a king! That's *Regent's Punch*, a favorite of the then prince regent of England who was to become George IV. A simplified, individual serving of this punch is given in chapter I.

🕯 | *Regent's Punch #2*

1 bottle Rhine wine
2 bottles Madeira
1 bottle orange curaçao
1 bottle Cognac
1 pint Jamaica rum
1 pint green tea
Juice of 10 oranges
Juice of 6 lemons
Sugar to taste
3 bottles champagne
2 bottles club soda
Orange and lemon slices

All ingredients should be prechilled. Blend everything but champagne, club soda, and garnish in a punch bowl with a large cake of ice. Immediately before serving, gently stir in champagne and club soda. Garnish with a few sliced oranges and lemons.

The following bevy of historic punches are all from another time and place. Some are well known and are fixtures in old mixer's manuals. We have tried to go to the source wherever possible, and in some cases we have modified recipes to appeal to modern tastes.

🕯 | *Cardinal Punch*

2 bottles red Bordeaux
1 pint cognac
1 pint Jamaica rum
4 oz. sweet vermouth
1 bottle champagne
2 quarts club soda
Sugar to taste

Prechill all ingredients and mix everything well in a punch bowl with a cake of ice, except soda and champagne, which should be added just before serving. Some prefer more champagne in place of club soda.

🦢 | *Lafayette Punch*

6 oranges, thinly sliced
Confectioners' sugar
2 bottles Mosel or
  California Johannesburg
  riesling
3 bottles brut champagne

Cover the bottom of a punch bowl with orange slices and lay down a heavy coating of sugar. Pour 1 bottle of Mosel over oranges and sugar and allow to ripen for at least 2 hours. Add a cake of ice and pour in another bottle of Mosel and 3 bottles of champagne. All wines should be thoroughly chilled in advance.

🦢 | *Race Day Cup*

½ cup lemon juice
½ cup cognac
2 oz. kirsch
½ oz. maraschino liqueur
1 pint club soda
Sugar to taste
Cucumber peel, sliced
Borage leaves (optional)
1 bottle brut champagne
Lemon slices and
  maraschino cherries

Prechill all ingredients and mix everything, except the champagne and garnish, in punch bowl with a block of ice. Add champagne just before serving. Remove cucumber peel after 30 minutes. Garnish with a *few* pieces of fruit, if you wish.

🦢 | *Bacchus Cup*

1 cup medium sherry
4 oz. cognac
1½ oz. crème de noyaux
1 bottle brut champagne
½ bottle club soda
Sugar to taste

Prechill all ingredients and mix in a punch bowl with a cake of ice. If a sweet sherry is used, omit sugar.

🎵 | Roman Punch

1 bottle Barbados rum
1 bottle champagne
½ oz. orange bitters
1 cup lemon juice
¾ cup orange juice
Sugar to taste
Whites of 10 eggs
Orange peel

Mix all ingredients, except egg whites and garnish, in a punch bowl with a cake of ice. Beat egg whites until peaks are fairly stiff and gently stir into punch. Garnish with orange peels cut in long strips.

🎵 | The Devil's Cup

1½ oz. yellow Chartreuse
1½ oz. green Chartreuse
1½ oz. Benedictine
4 oz. cognac
2 bottles brut champagne
4 oz. lemon juice (optional)
1 bottle club soda
    (optional)

Prechill all ingredients and mix in a punch bowl with a block of ice. Some prefer to add lemon juice for tartness or club soda for dilution.

🎵 | Balaklava Cup

4 oz. lemon juice
Peel of 2 lemons, grated
2 bottles red Burgundy or
    Bordeaux
Sugar to taste
Cucumber peel, sliced
Borage leaves (optional)
3 bottles brut champagne

Prechill all ingredients and mix everything except the champagne in a punch bowl with a block of ice. Add champagne just before serving. Cucumber should be removed after about 30 minutes. (*Note:* Borage is an herb that was popular in punch a hundred years ago.)

🕭 | *Napoleon Punch*

1 bottle red Burgundy
1 cup gold label Puerto
  Rican rum
1-lb. can dark sweet pitted
  cherries
1 tbsp. vanilla extract
1 bottle club soda or
  sparkling Burgundy
4 oz. maraschino liqueur

Pour prechilled Burgundy and rum into a punch bowl. Drain juice from cherries and add to bowl along with vanilla extract and soda or sparkling Burgundy. Sweeten with maraschino to taste. Garnish with canned cherries. Add cake of ice.

According to Edward Spencer, whose classic work *The Flowing Bowl* is a repository of much wisdom concerning the proper use and enjoyment of wines and spirits and a source for many hoary recipes, *Halo Punch* was another potation dear to the heart of the prince regent of England in the days before he was crowned George IV.

🕭 | *Halo Punch*

Sugar cubes
1 lemon
2 oranges
1 cup boiling water
½ pint pineapple syrup
1 pint strong green tea
1 pint cognac
½ pint Barbados rum
2 bottles champagne

Use as many sugar cubes as are needed to rub off all of the zest (outer peel) from lemon and oranges. Put cubes into a punch bowl with juice and pulp from fruit. Add boiling water and stir until all sugar is dissolved. Mix in syrup, tea, cognac, and rum and a cake of ice. Pour in chilled champagne immediately before serving.

In days of old, a loving cup was a multihandled affair that was passed among the guests to mark an auspicious occasion such as a leave-taking, a victory, or an anniversary. This old recipe was ostensibly a concoction considered suitable for these important events.

❧ | *Loving Cup*

4 lemons
Sugar cubes
Lemon balm (optional)
Borage leaves (optional)
1 bottle Madeira
1 pint cognac
2 bottles champagne

Rub the peels of lemons vigorously with as many sugar cubes as are needed to completely remove all of the zest (outside layer of peel). Squeeze juice from lemons and pour into a punch bowl with sugar cubes, add a quart of water or club soda, herbs (if available), Madeira, and cognac. Let mixture steep for a few hours, then add a cake of ice and stir in chilled champagne. (*Note*: Since borage imparts a cucumber flavor, cucumber peel may be used as a substitute. This recipe can also be made with fresh mint. Be sure to bruise the leaves to release the essential oil. Balm was popular in medieval times as a wine drink additive.)

The following elegant old punch requires orgeat syrup, which is made from almonds and imparts a rich flavor to drinks of all kinds, and makes an excellent substitute for sugar in punches, tropical rum drinks, and cocktails. Orgeat can be purchased at stores specializing in gourmet foods.

🐚 | Crimean Cup

6 lemons
Scant tsp. sugar
1 quart club soda
1 pint cognac
1 pint Jamaica rum
4 oz. maraschino liqueur
Orgeat syrup to taste
2 bottles champagne

Cut the outer peel (zest) from the lemons and place in a mortar with sugar to bruise the peels with a pestle, extracting oil. Transfer to a punch bowl. Pour in cold club soda and mix well; then mix in cognac, rum, maraschino, and juice from the lemons. Add enough orgeat to sweeten and place a block of ice in bowl. Immediately before serving, add chilled champagne. Add additional club soda if you wish.

Punches have always been popular on shipboard, where the community cocktail bowl offers an expeditious means of quenching the thirst of all hands and an opportunity for socializing. *Old Navy Punch* will make old sea dogs sit up and beg for more.

🐚 | Old Navy Punch

Juice of 4 lemons
1 fresh pineapple
1 pint Jamaica rum
1 pint cognac
1 pint peach brandy
1 pint orange curaçao
Sugar or Falernum to taste
4 bottles champagne

Put juice of lemons and their peels into a punch bowl. Cut ripe pineapple into cubes about a half an inch in size. Crush half of the cubes and put into bowl with juice. Add rum, cognac, peach brandy, and curaçao; sweeten to taste with sugar or Falernum. Add a block of ice and mix well. Immediately before serving, stir in chilled champagne (*Note*: Falernum is a flavored syrup from Barbados and is highly recommended for sweetening punches and rum drinks.)

A PROLIFERATION OF PUNCHES

This recipe comes from the old and honorable St. Cecelia Society of Charleston, South Carolina. This punch, which is both authoritative and delicious, is a variation on another eighteenth-century recipe: Fish House Punch, which utilizes brandy, rum, peach brandy, lemon juice, sugar, and spring water in place of champagne.

🦢 | St. Cecelia Society Punch

8 lemons and limes, mixed and thinly sliced

1 fresh pineapple thinly sliced or 1 cup pineapple juice

Confectioners' sugar, to taste

1 bottle cognac

1 bottle peach brandy

1 pint Jamaica rum

1 quart green tea

4 bottles brut champagne

1–2 quarts club soda

The day before the party, cover the bottom of a large container with lemon, lime, and pineapple slices, spread a generous amount of sugar over fruit and pummel gently with a muddler. Add cognac, peach brandy, and rum; cover tightly and set aside at room temperature. Several hours before serving, transfer to a punch bowl with a block of ice and add tea. Immediately before serving, gently stir in chilled champagne and a quart or two of cold club soda. Garnish with a few fresh lemon and lime slices.

Volume II of *The Gentleman's Companion*, by Charles H. Baker, Jr., is the best book on exotic drinks I have ever encountered. Written with great flair and filled with anecdotes and historical tidbits, it is a fascinating account of the author's travels about the world "with jigger, beaker, and flask." During my travels in India, on occasion I was served refreshing champagne punches, which were purportedly authentic *Bengal Lancer's Punch*. I reacted with the exultation a visitor to the United States might exhibit on being served an "absolutely authentic mint julep." Mr. Baker's recipe tastes *absolutely* authentic to me, and I highly recommend it.

🐉 | Bengal Lancer's Punch

½ cup orange juice
½ cup pineapple juice
½ cup lime juice
3 oz. Barbados rum
3 oz. curaçao
1 liter red Bordeaux
Sugar to taste
1 liter champagne
1 pint club soda
Lime slices

Prechill all ingredients and mix everything, except champagne, soda, and garnish, in a punch bowl with a cake of ice. Immediately before serving, stir in champagne and club soda. Garnish with a few lime slices.

Another famous military stirrup cup is *Dragoon Punch*, which, like many recipes for Wassail, is a curious mixture of wines and brewage that comes to us from ancient times. Porter is a dark, rich, fermented beverage that is best described as being something in between ale and stout. If porter is unavailable, you may use a couple of pints of Guinness stout.

🐉 | Dragoon Punch

2 lemons, thinly sliced
Sugar
6 oz. cognac
6 oz. sherry
1 quart ale
1 quart porter
1 quart champagne

Prechill all ingredients. Arrange sliced lemons in a punch bowl and cover with sugar; bruise fruit with a muddler. Mix in all ingredients with a block of ice, but save champagne until last. Immediately before serving stir champagne in gently.

From a historical perspective perhaps the most prestigious of all champagne punches is the libation that George Washington served at a farewell party for his officers at Fraunces Tavern in New York City on December 4, 1783. Washington gave not one but two memorable fêtes that year. The first was a victory celebration that he hosted for his staff and regimental commanders shortly after the British surrender. It must have been some party, for it is recorded that his celebration took its toll in 108 bottles of Madeira and port, consumed, and "8 lights, 16 wine glasses, and 6 decanters" broken.

At the December farewell party, which was held in the famous Long Room on the second floor of the tavern, Washington produced his own recipe for what he described as a "brandy toddy." Here is the original recipe for what was purported to be a great favorite at Mount Vernon.

Brew a pint of strong lemonade. Add thereto a half pint of apricot brandy and one pint of Cognac. Stir these ingredients together and pour the concoction over a piece of ice that has been placed in the punch bowl. Just before serving, add two quarts of chilled Champagne and dress the bowl with fresh mint leaves, sliced oranges and seasonable fruits.

Provided that sugar is added, the recipe is quite usable without modification. American soldiers were to rediscover this fine drink, in a slightly different form, in France during World War I, where cognac and champagne became famous as the French 75 (see Chapter I).

Now follows a variety of champagne punches of recent vintage, selected for their imaginative use of fresh fruits in flavor combinations consonant with modern tastes. Our thanks to the friendly folks at the Wine Institute in San Francisco and the Champagne News and Information Bureau in New York City, who supplied some of the recipes. While traditional punch recipes have undergone a renaissance among younger drinkers in recent years, new punches have also been created. These recipes follow the general trend to more fresh fruits and natural ingredients *sans* preservatives, additives, artificial flavors and colors, etc.—although, as we have seen, it is difficult to imagine any commodity that is subjected to more chemical additives than wine—and many of the new recipes produce punches that are brisk, bright, zesty, and refreshing. A sampling follows:

🔊 | Champagne Bowle

1 grapefruit, sectioned
3 oranges or tangerines, sectioned
1 small, ripe pineapple, diced
2 ripe bananas, peeled and thinly sliced
1 cup Jamaica rum
2 oz. triple sec
2 oz. kirsch
2 oz. grenadine
2 bottles brut champagne
Fresh mint sprigs (optional)

Mix all ingredients, except champagne and mint, in a covered bowl and refrigerate for several hours. Transfer to a punch bowl, add a block of ice, and pour in chilled champagne just before serving. Garnish with mint sprigs. (*Note*: A *few* of the fruit sections may be crushed to release juices, but don't overdo.)

🔊 | Cranberry Champagne Punch

1 pint cranberry juice
Juice of 1 grapefruit
Juice of half a lime
1 cup gin
Maple syrup or honey to taste
1–2 bottles of champagne
Maraschino cherries
Orange peel

Mix all ingredients, except champagne and garnishes, in a punch bowl with a large cake of ice. Just before serving, add 1 to 2 bottles of chilled champagne and garnish with cherries and orange peel.

🍷 | *Fiesta Champagne Punch*

1 quart raspberry sherbet
  or sorbet
4 oz. framboise
2 oz. orange curaçao
2 bottles champagne
1 cup fresh raspberries

Blend sherbet, framboise, and curaçao in a punch bowl with a cake of ice. Immediately before serving, pour in chilled champagne and stir gently. Garnish with fresh raspberries.

🍷 | *Champagne Punch aux Fraises*

1 quart strawberries,
  pureed
Cucumber peel, cut in a
  thick spiral
2–4 oz. apricot liqueur
2 bottles brut champagne
1 dozen whole strawberries
  with caps on

Mix pureed strawberries, cucumber peel, and apricot liqueur in a bowl; chill for several hours. Transfer to a punch bowl with a cake of ice. Immediately before serving, gently stir in chilled champagne; add whole strawberries.

🍷 | *Champagne Punch Colette*

1½ cups bar-le-duc (red
  currants in syrup)
1 pint rosé wine
2 bottles brut champagne
Lemon and lime slices
Fresh mint sprigs (optional)

In a small bowl mix bar-le-duc and rosé; chill for several hours. Transfer to a punch bowl with a cake of ice and pour in chilled champagne just before serving. Garnish with a few lemon and lime slices and sprigs of mint.

❧ California Champagne Punch

2 cups peaches, sliced
2 cups melon balls
2 cups strawberries, sliced
Lemon juice
Sugar to taste
2 bottles California Chablis
2 bottles California
champagne

Place fruits in a bowl and sprinkle well with lemon juice and sugar. Add Chablis and refrigerate for several hours. Transfer to a punch bowl, add a block of ice, and pour in chilled champagne immediately before serving.

❧ Champagne Tokay Punch

2 pints sweet Tokay (Tokaji
Aszu)
1 small can frozen lemon
juice
1–2 bottles brut
champagne
Lemon or lime slices

Blend chilled Tokay with lemon juice in a punch bowl with a cake of ice. Just before serving, gently stir in cold champagne and garnish with a few lemon or lime slices. (*Note*: You will need a fairly sweet Tokay to bring this off. Genuine Hungarian Tokay is not cheap, but the result justifies the cost.)

Sangría, the red wine and fruit punch of Spanish origin that has become so popular in the United States, is one of the great success stories of the punch renaissance. Sangría rode to success as a part of the wine boom that began in this country in the early 1960s (in some parts of the United States it started even earlier). The popularity of sangría in Spain almost certainly began with the planting of grapes by the Romans in ancient times. In America, some wine historians believe that it all began at the New York World's Fair of 1964–65. Anyone who was fortunate enough to visit the Spanish Pavilion—one of the fair's real attractions—will remember people standing in line for sangría (just as they did at the Belgian Pavilion, where thick, munchy Belgian waffles were the rage. But then, waffles have always been an American staple). However, little did we suspect at the time that this Spanish red wine punch had such a bright future on these shores.

One of the reasons for sangría's success is that it is cheap, easy to make, and very refreshing. It can be thrown together in seconds, and uses ingredients that are readily available and a red wine that might be very close to being undrinkable under other circumstances. And so American wine drinkers learned indirectly what purveyors of cheap wines have known for a thousand years: If a wine is harsh and unpleasant to drink, douse it with sugar and serve it crackling cold.

❧ | Party Sangría

1 bottle red wine
1 lemon or lime, thinly
    sliced
1 orange, thinly sliced
1½ oz. triple sec
1½ oz. brandy (optional)
12-oz. bottle club soda
Sugar to taste

Prechill all ingredients, except club soda and sugar, and mix in a punch bowl with a block of ice. Add club soda just before serving and stir gently. Squeeze juice from additional lemons, limes, or oranges and add to punch if you want more fruit flavor. Add sugar to taste.

Sangría means "bleeding" in Spanish (from *sangre*, the Spanish word for blood), and although the connection with red wine is obvious, not all sangrías must be made with red wine. Here are some blond sangrías.

❧ | *Sangría Blondo*

1 bottle Chablis or
   Johannesburg riesling
Juice of 1 lemon or 2 limes
Juice of 1 orange
1 oz. orange curaçao
Several dashes of kirsch
Sugar to taste
12-oz. bottle club soda
Peel from lemon or limes
Peel from orange

Prechill all ingredients, and mix everything, except club soda and garnishes, in a punch bowl with a cake of ice. Pour in soda just before serving; stir gently. Then garnish with lemon, lime, and orange peel.

❧ | *Champagne Sangría*

1 bottle Mosel or
   Johannesburg riesling
2 limes, thinly sliced
1 cup grapefruit sections
1 oz. triple sec
2 oz. gin
Sugar to taste
1 bottle champagne
Fresh mint (optional)

Prechill all ingredients and mix in a punch bowl with a block of ice, saving champagne until ready to serve. Squeeze juice from additional grapefruit sections and add to punch. Garnish with fresh mint, if you wish.

🐌 | *Strawberry Blond Sangría*

1 cup frozen strawberries in syrup
1 lemon or lime, thinly sliced
1 orange, thinly sliced
1 bottle dry white wine
½ cup sloe gin or strawberry liqueur
Several dashes of kirsch
Sugar to taste
12-oz. bottle club soda

Prechill all ingredients. Blend frozen strawberries with syrup in punch bowl with fruit slices, wine, sloe gin, and kirsch, and sweeten to taste. Add a cake of ice and pour in club soda just before serving. For more citrus flavor, squeeze juice from additional lemons, limes, and oranges and stir into punch, if you wish.

Here are a few other variations on the basic Spanish sangría that rely heavily upon fruits for their flavor.

🐌 | *Sparkling Burgundy Sangría*

½ cup pineapple juice
½ cup orange juice
Juice of 1 lime or lemon
1 small can apricots
½ cup apple brandy or cognac
2 oz. kirsch
Sugar to taste
2 bottles sparkling Burgundy
Orange and lime peel

Prechill all ingredients. Blend everything, except Burgundy and citrus peels, together in a punch bowl. Bruise apricots to release some of the flavor and allow to stand for 30 minutes before adding ice cake. Pour in chilled Burgundy, and stir gently immediately before serving. Garnish with orange and lime peels that have been cut in long spirals.

🐚 Fruit Cup Sangría

2 10-oz. packages frozen
  mixed fruit in syrup
4 oz. lemon juice
6 oz. grapefruit juice
4 oz. cherry liqueur
4 oz. blackberry brandy
4 oz. orange curaçao
2 liters dry red wine
2 quarts club soda
1 orange and 1 lemon,
  thinly sliced

Prechill all ingredients and blend everything, except club soda and fruit slices, in a punch bowl with a block of ice. Immediately before serving, gently stir in club soda and garnish with a few orange and lemon slices. (*Note*: Syrup from frozen fruits should provide sufficient sweetening.)

🐚 Janet Street's Sangría

12-oz. can pear nectar
12-oz. can apricot nectar
Juice of 1 lemon
1 cup brandy
1 cup triple sec
2 bottles dry red wine
2 quarts club soda
Orange and lemons, thinly
  sliced

Prechill all liquid ingredients. Mix everything, except club soda and fruit slices, together in a punch bowl with a cake of ice. Immediately before serving, gently stir in club soda and garnish with a few thin lemon and orange slices. (*Note*: Sugar should not be needed as fruit nectars and triple sec should add enough sweetening.)

Punches can be anything you want them to be, and many punches that are quite palatable contain no wine at all but are mixtures of fruits, spirits, and a sweetener; they may or may not include other flavorings such as spices and herbs. Fish House Punch, that venerable libation born with the Republic, is a case in point: It is a deliciously balanced mixture of cognac, rum, peach brandy, lemon juice, sugar, and spring water. The addition of champagne in place of water turns it into true ambrosia, and a potent cup for the gods, to be sure. But then, as our forefathers knew so well, punch was never designed to be gulped like beer or quaffed like whiskey, but sipped and savored as an accompaniment to jovial conversation and the trading of wit and laughter. The remainder of the punches presented here are a mixture of old and new. They have been selected not only because they taste good, but because wine is their reason for being, and they would not be nearly so tempting and satisfying if they were made without it.

The *Claret Cup* is a fixture in many bartender's guides. Here is a good representative recipe.

૨⚫ | Claret Cup

1½–2 cups mixed fruits of your choice (orange, grapefruit sections, berries, sliced peaches, apricots, pears, etc.)
6 oz. cognac
6 oz. maraschino liqueur
6 oz. triple sec
2 oz. kirsh or framboise
Juice of 1 lemon (optional)
2 bottles Bordeaux or California cabernet sauvignon
1 quart club soda (optional)

Prechill all ingredients and mix everything, except club soda, in a bowl. Cover tightly and let stand for a few hours in a cool place. Pour into a punch bowl with a block of ice and add soda just before serving, if you wish.

The following Claret Cup variations have been selected because their interesting flavor combinations enhance the taste of red wine.

🍂 | *Sparkling Claret Cup*

1 cup cognac
½ cup orange curaçao
2 oz. maraschino liqueur
2 bottles Bordeaux or
  California cabernet
  sauvignon
2 bottles sparkling Mosel
  or 1 bottle sparkling
  Mosel and 1 bottle club
  soda
Lemon and orange peel

Prechill all ingredients and blend everything, except sparkling wine, soda, and citrus peels, in a punch bowl with a cake of ice. Just before serving, gently stir in sparkling wine and soda. (*Note*: Some old punch recipes call for a sparkling wine *and* club soda, which may seem redundant. The purpose was to smooth out the punch, give it effervescence without adding to the alcoholic content.) Garnish with lemon and orange peel.

🍂 | *Ascot Cup*

1 pint dry sherry
½ cup orange curaçao
½ cup cognac
½ cup raspberry syrup
Several dashes of framboise
½ cup lemon juice
Sugar to taste
2 bottles Bordeaux or
  California cabernet
  sauvignon
1–2 quarts club soda
1 orange and 1 lemon,
  thinly sliced

Prechill all ingredients and mix everything, except club soda and citrus slices, in a punch bowl with a cake of ice. Stir in club soda just before serving and garnish with a few slices of orange and lemon.

Burgundy, generally a robust, full-bodied red wine, and its first cousin, the pinot noir of California, make sturdy, authoritative

A PROLIFERATION OF PUNCHES

punches because the wines are strong enough to survive mixing with many diverse ingredients—such as port and cherry brandy as in the recipe below.

🦢 | *Chevalier Punch*

½ cup lemon juice
1 cup orange juice
1 pint ruby port
1½ cups cherry brandy or
  ½ cup kirsch and 1 cup
  cherry liqueur
2 liters Burgundy or pinot
  noir
8½-oz. can dark, sweet
  cherries
1 quart club soda
  (optional)
Orange and lemon peel

Prechill all ingredients and blend everything, except cherries, club soda, and citrus peels, in a punch bowl with a block of ice. Pour in cherries with juice, and just before serving, stir in club soda and garnish with a few orange and lemon peels. (*Note*: If cherry liqueur is used, no additional sugar should be needed.)

Rum and wine make a good punch combination for those who prefer a cheering cup that is strong and bracing.

🦢 | *Burgundy Bishop*

Juice of 1 lemon or lime
½ cup Barbados rum
1 oz. cognac
1 bottle Burgundy or pinot
  noir
Sugar to taste
Orange peel cut in a spiral

Prechill all ingredients and blend well in a punch bowl with a cake of ice. Garnish with orange peel.

🐌 | Buddha Punch

¾ cup orange juice
½ cup lemon juice
½ cup orange curaçao
Several dashes kirsch
½ cup amber Puerto Rican
   rum
Several dashes of
   Angostura Bitters
Falernum or sugar to taste
1 pint Rhine wine
1 bottle sparkling Mosel or
   champagne
Fresh mint (optional)

Prechill all ingredients and mix everything, except sparkling wine and mint,
in a punch bowl with a cake of ice. Just
before serving, stir in sparkling wine
and garnish with mint.

A modern version of an old favorite has been relabeled the *Velvet Hammer*.

🐌 | Velvet Hammer

Juice of 2 limes
¾ cup amber Puerto Rican
   rum
½ cup strong tea
1 bottle sauterne
Sugar to taste
Several dashes orange
   bitters (optional)
Lime peel

Prechill all ingredients and mix in a
punch bowl with a cake of ice. Garnish
with lime peel cut into strips.

A pleasant variation of the rum-wine punch combination is this pleasant teatime recipe that comes from Jamaica.

🐌 | *Blue Mountain Punch*

Juice of 2 limes
½ cup orange juice
½ cup cognac
3 oz. Jamaica rum
1 oz. triple sec
1 liter Chablis
1 quart club soda
Orange and lime peel

Prechill all ingredients and mix everything, except club soda and citrus peels, in a punch bowl with a cake of ice. Just before serving, pour in club soda and garnish with orange and lime peel cut in strips.

Rhine Wine Punch is one of the great old classics, and nearly everybody has his own special favorite recipe. This is a distillation of the best of many good formulations.

🐌 | *Rhine Wine Punch*

1 pint lemon juice
1 cup cognac
1 cup strong tea
½ cup maraschino liqueur
1 pint oloroso sherry
Honey to taste
Cucumber peel
3 bottles Rhine wine
1 quart club soda
Lemon peel

Prechill all ingredients and mix everything, except club soda and lemon peel, in a punch bowl with a cake of ice. After 30 minutes remove cucumber peel; gently stir in club soda and garnish with lemon peel cut in strips. (*Note:* If you want a sweet punch, use cream sherry; a drier punch, fino sherry. Oloroso is on the sweet side.)

Here are some old recipes popular in the days when the wines from the Rhine and Mosel areas were called "hock," especially in England, where the white wines grown in the vicinity of Hockheim were much revered.

🦢 Pineapple Hock Cup

1 fresh pineapple, very ripe, or frozen pineapple chunks
¾ cup orange juice
½ cup gin
2 oz. maraschino liqueur
Raspberry syrup to taste (or you may, in a pinch, use grenadine)
1 bottle sparkling Mosel or Saumur

Prechill all ingredients and mix everything, except the sparkling wine, in a punch bowl with a cake of ice. The pineapple should be cut or diced into small pieces to release juice. Pour in wine just before serving. (*Note*: If you need more liquid, add more wine.)

🦢 Hock Punch

Juice of 1 lemon
½ cup B&B liqueur
2 oz. Grand Marnier
2 oz. yellow Chartreuse
1 bottle Rhine wine or California Johannesburg riesling
1 pint club soda
Cucumber and lemon peel
Mint sprigs (optional)

Prechill all ingredients and blend everything, except club soda, lemon peel, and mint in a punch bowl with a cake of ice. After 30 minutes remove cucumber peel. Pour in soda when ready to serve; garnish with lemon peel and mint sprigs.

A *shrub* is a mixture of fruit, sugar, water, and spirits put up to mature for a nominal period of time, usually not more than two months. The advantage of this aged punch is that the maturation process allows the flavor of fruit and spirit to marry. This is exactly what is done with many punches made in the bowl, when the ingredients are allowed to stand for an hour or so, or sometimes overnight, before serving. Here is an old recipe.

🐚 | *Queen Anne's Shrub*

1 pint lemon juice
Grated zest (outer peel) of
    4 lemons
2 lbs. sugar or honey
2 bottles brandy
2 bottles dry white wine
Lemon peel cut in spirals
Fresh mint

In a suitable container with a tight-fitting lid mix lemon juice, lemon zest, and sugar or honey together until well blended. Add both bottles of brandy and 1 bottle of wine. Seal the container and put in a cool place for 5 to 6 weeks, after which it should be ready. To serve, strain and pour all or a part of the shrub into a punch bowl with a cake of ice and add second bottle of wine. Garnish with fresh lemon peel and mint.

As we have seen, the practice of steeping herbs in wine is one hallowed by a good many thousands of years' tradition. In the spirit world, the placing of mint in a glass with bourbon and water to produce a mint julep is a well-known custom. So is the use of woodruff or *Waldmeister* to make what is popularly called "May wine."

🐚 | *May Wine Bowle*

6–8 bunches fresh
    woodruff or 1 cup dried
    woodruff
½ lb. sugar
1 cup cognac
3–4 bottles Rhine wine
1–2 bottles champagne or
    club soda
1 cup fresh, whole
    strawberries

Place woodruff in a container with a tight-fitting cover and add sugar, a bottle of Rhine wine and cognac; let stand in a cool place overnight or place in refrigerator. If dried woodruff is used, you will need to put it in a cheesecloth bag. Transfer to a large punch bowl with a block of ice and pour in rest of the Rhine wine and several bottles of champagne or club soda. Wine should be well chilled before adding to bowl . Garnish with fresh strawberries.

And now a gathering of punches and punch-type drinks that reflect modern tastes through the use of convenience products and offbeat combinations—all of which attest to the versatility of wine as an essential ingredient in mixed drinks.

From Sweden comes an unusual, but very satisfying, concoction called *Inez Punch*, which is presented here as an individual cup. The other recipes make enough for group consumption.

ঽ৯ | *Inez Punch*

2 oz. orange juice
2 oz. cabernet sauvignon
1 oz. cream sherry
1 oz. vodka
1 oz. brandy
1 oz. Swedish Punch
  liqueur
Sugar to taste

Mix all ingredients in a blender with cracked ice and serve in chilled cocktail glasses.
SERVES 2.

ঽ৯ | *Dubonnet Punch*

Juice of 6 limes
1 pint gin or vodka
4 oz. orange curaçao
1 bottle Dubonnet
Lime peel cut in a spiral
Orange peel cut in a spiral
1 pint club soda

Prechill all ingredients and mix everything, except club soda, in a punch bowl with a cake of ice. Pour in club soda just before serving. Depending on strength desired, add additional soda, if you wish. Garnish with orange peel.

🐚 White Cargo

1 cup gin or vodka
2 oz. maraschino liqueur
1 quart vanilla ice cream
1 bottle sauterne

Prechill all ingredients and mix gently in a *chilled* punch bowl. Serve in chilled cups with spoons. If more sweetness is desired, add additional maraschino.

Here is an original that was created for Steve Allen, a longtime friend.

🐚 The Steverino

1 oz. pineapple juice
2 oz. California cabernet
sauvignon
1 oz. vodka
Several dashes of triple sec

Mix all ingredients in a blender with cracked ice and pour into a chilled cocktail glass. If more sweetness is desired, add more triple sec.
SERVES 1.

From the bar in the Hotel du Palais in Biarritz, France, comes this unusual drink.

🐚 Rayon Vert

2 oz. dry vermouth
1 oz. Izarra
1 oz. blue curaçao
Dash of orange curaçao
Dash of framboise

Mix all ingredients in a blender with cracked ice and serve in a chilled cocktail glass.
SERVES 1.

Lest rosé wine buffs feel that they have been given short shrift in these pages, I present three refreshing punches featuring the excellent rosé wines from France's beautiful Côtes de Provence.

₰ | *Provence Punch*

½ pint lemon juice
3 bottles Côtes de Provence
rosé
Sugar to taste
1–2 quarts 7-Up
Oranges and lemons, thinly
sliced

Prechill all ingredients and blend everything, except 7-Up and fruit slices, in a punch bowl with a cake of ice. Just before serving, pour in 7-Up and garnish with orange and lemon slices.

₰ | *Rosé Cup*

4 oz. bourbon
2 oz. orange curaçao
2 oz. Benedictine
1½ bottles Côtes de
Provence rosé
Sugar to taste
1 pint club soda
Orange slices

Prechill all ingredients and blend everything, except club soda and orange slices, in a punch bowl with a cake of ice. Just before serving, pour in club soda; garnish with orange slices.

₰ | *Cache*

1 oz. cherry liqueur
4 oz. Côtes de Provence
rosé
Tonic water
Lemon slice
Mint sprig

Prechill all ingredients and pour cherry liqueur and rosé into a tall Collins glass (with a little ice, if you wish); fill up with tonic water. Garnish with lemon slice and mint sprig.
SERVES 1.

A New England fisherman who loves coolers and punches made of cranberry juice and various wines sent us the recipe for *Rosy Cranberry Punch*. "On a hot day after working on the dock, there's nothing better than a big, ice-cold pitcher of cranberry juice and sauterne mixed half and half, unless it's rosy cranberry punch—a great favorite hereabouts."

ટ✿ | *Rosy Cranberry Punch*

2 6-oz. cans orange, orange-pineapple, or pineapple juice (frozen concentrate)
1 quart cranberry juice cocktail
1 bottle Mateus rosé (750 ml.)

Pour juice concentrate, prechilled cranberry juice, and wine into a bowl or pitcher, with or without ice, or mix in an electric blender.

And one more rosé punch: this one from the seaport city of Marsala from which the rich, fortified wine of Sicily takes its name.

ટ✿ | *Marsala Punch*

½ cup lemon juice
½ cup orange juice
1 bottle bourbon or brandy
2 bottles rosé
2 bottles Marsala
2 oz. triple sec
1 orange and 1 lemon, thinly sliced

Prechill all ingredients and mix well in a punch bowl with a cake of ice. Garnish with orange and lemon slices.

Finally, a few oddball concoctions for those adventurous souls who have tired of the conventional and the traditional punch formulations or who enjoy trying new taste experiences. *Ginger Wine Punch* is certainly a new taste episode for most Americans, although it has enjoyed a certain amount of popularity in England.

🐌 | *Ginger Wine Punch*

1 pint apple cider
1 pint grapefruit juice
1 pint pineapple juice
Juice of 1 lemon
1 bottle applejack or
   calvados
1 bottle brandy or bourbon
2 bottles green ginger wine
Honey or maple syrup to
   taste
1 quart ginger beer, ginger
   ale, or club soda
1 apple, diced

Prechill all ingredients and blend everything, except apple, in a punch bowl with a cake of ice. Garnish with diced apple or very thin apple slices.

One of my all-time favorite wine drinks is a punch of sorts without peer as a great restorative to mind and body and very flavorful to boot. I was introduced to this by our Scottish gillie while shooting in Perthshire one bone-chilling, wet, soggy November. At the end of the last drive, which produced nothing more than frostbitten fingers and faces (the grouse were much too smart to be out and about in such dreary weather), a flask of *Shooting Mixture* was produced. From the first bracing swig, a remarkable transformation took place. It made our blood race, brought feeling back to our benumbed limbs, and gave us renewed will to survive the rigors of Scottish winter weather. It is highly recommended as a restorative after all outdoor activities in the cold.

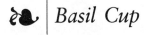

Shooting Mixture

3 pints cherry wine
1½ pints cherry brandy
1 pint cognac

Mix all ingredients in exactly the same proportions given in the recipe whether making a small amount or enough for a regiment. Shooting Mixture may be bottled for future use and will keep well if stored in a cool place. Another version of this drink calls for the substitution of sloe wine for cherry wine, gin in place of cherry brandy, and sloe gin instead of cognac.

From the Wine Institute in San Francisco comes this very unusual recipe. Although not strictly speaking a punch, it can be served as one.

Basil Cup

1 cup sweet basil leaves
1 liter California muscatel
Lemon juice
Lemon slices

Wash a generous cup of fresh basil leaves, bruise slightly to release flavor, and steep leaves in wine for 3 or 4 hours. Strain and pour into a bowl or individual glasses with ice and add a dash or two of lemon juice for accent. Garnish with lemon slices.

It is hoped that this collection of punches will provide sufficient instruction to ensure your reputation as someone who provides amply for his or her guests, and that you will be inspired to bring friends and family into the magic circle that surrounds the flowing bowl. It has been a wellspring of good cheer, happy times, and fast friendships from ancient times. It is one hallowed institution that deserves to continue.

IV | ARTISTRY WITH APERITIFS

As you no doubt know, *apéritif* is a French word for almost anything liquid consumed as a refreshment before meals. Thus, the gastronomically innovative French were enjoying the "Happy Hour" a century or more before the American Cocktail Hour was devised to bridge that limbo period between the end of the work day and the beginning of dinner. (It was called "The Black Half Hour" in the old days, when everyone would sit around making small talk, twiddling their thumbs, or listening to the wireless, waiting for dinner to be served.) The word *apéritif* comes from the Latin *aperio*, which means "to open," and since the Romans were given to making wine concoctions of all kinds, some of which were taken before as well as during meals, we must give them credit for this most civilized custom—along with the Greeks, whose penchant for introducing the odd and the unusual into their potations we have already discussed.

Although aperitifs, like cocktails, can describe almost anything alcoholic, here we are primarily concerned with a broad category best described as "aromatized wines." These are wine-based mixtures containing various botanicals (herbs, spices, fruits, and other diverse flavorings) fortified with alcohol to bring them up to a level of approximately 18 percent alcohol by volume—although some have levels as low as 15 percent or as high as 21 percent. We will not dwell here on the many liquors that are drunk as aperitifs, such as gin, vodka, whiskey, cognac, and the like; or bitter drams such as Amer Picon, Campari, or Fernet Branca; or the those licorice-tasting spirits such as Pernod, Ricard, ouzo, or arack so beloved by Mediterranean peoples, *except* as companionable and necessary ingredients in wine-based mixed drinks. Perhaps the finest aperitif of them all, champagne, along with champagne-type sparkling wines, has been treated in another part of this book.

* * *

Vermouth is one of the most popular and widely used alcoholic beverages in the world today. In America, we think of it as a rather trivial ingredient in the martini, Manhattan, or Rob Roy cocktail, or perhaps a light refreshment mixed with cassis or on the rocks with a twist. The truth is that vermouth is specified as an ingredient in more mixed drinks found in all the old bartender's guides than any other single ingredient (gin being a close second). Classified as a fortified wine, vermouth is in actuality much more than that. Vermouth is a complex spirit that epitomizes the blender's art. Not only a great flavor catalyst, it is also a versatile modifier that mixes and blends with almost any ingredient used to make a cocktail. Hence its popularity as a cocktail ingredient *par excellence*. And there is a very good reason for this. It is because vermouth contains so many additives—as many as forty in some brands—that superb blending is essential in turning out a product that is balanced and that has character. All of the great vermouth houses in Italy and France have had plenty of opportunity to practice. Antonio Benedetto Carpano of Turin is generally credited with being the first to market an aromatized wine under the name vermouth; this was in 1776, an auspicious year. Carlo Stefano and Giovanni Giacomo Cinzano had been making aromatized wines under their own name since 1757. Since all proprietary vermouth formulas are closely guarded secrets and nobody born in the eighteenth century divulged the secret, we'll never know if the original products of Carpano and Cinzano were similar. As to the origin of the word *vermouth*, it comes from the German *wermut*, which means "wormwood," an additive that was used to spice up German rieslings beginning in the sixteenth century, or possibly even earlier. And where did the Germans learn to perk up their wine with all manner of blossoms, leaves, roots, barks, fruits, seeds, and such? From the Romans, of course, who planted their vineyards in the pre-Christian era. And so we come full circle in the timeless story of wine, man's constant companion since scribes put stylus to papyrus—and probably long before.

Many Europeans and South Americans take vermouth straight or with a little ice. The Italians drink enormous amounts of Cinzano and Martini & Rossi sweet vermouth, so much so that all the old bar guides refer to sweet vermouth as "Italian vermouth." Vermouth is also very popular in France, and despite the fact that dry vermouth made by Noilly Prat & Co. of Marseilles is widely used in the United States (along with Boissiere, Cinzano, and Martini & Rossi dry vermouths) as an ingredient in the redoubtable dry martini and the so-called "perfect" Manhattan and Rob Roy (equal parts of both sweet and dry vermouth instead of just one of the other), my impression, after indefatigably touring many watering places, is that educated French palates lean toward the red vermouths, which have more assertive flavors than their paler cousins. A particular favorite is Chambraise, an intriguing vermouth with the elusive flavor of wild strawberries. Another outstanding vermouth is Punt e Mes, meaning a "point and a half," a possible allusion to a local stockbroker who ordered his vermouth and shouted out his bid in the same breath. This bittersweet vermouth is made by G. B. Carpano of Turin, the same firm that made the original "spirit of '76." Two other vermouths are, to my mind, in a class by themselves. Both are "white goods" (pale straw would perhaps be more accurate), but should not to be confused with the traditional dry vermouths. Their flavors are much more complex and interesting, and they are excellent when served, well chilled, from the bottle. Lillet, made by Lillet Frères of Podensac, France, has a subtle, captivating flavor of herbs and spices, with just enough Armagnac to add the right amount of zest. While Lillet also comes in a red version, I prefer the pale variety. Cinzano, that fine old company that has placed triangular ashtrays with the big red-white-and-blue labels in every bar, bistro, and café in Europe, makes a mellow, piquant, medium-sweet vermouth called Cinzano Bianco. It is also straw-colored with a flavor more interesting than conventional dry vermouth, yet not as heavy as sweet vermouth.

American tastes being what they are—eclectic, pragmatic, down to earth, slightly irreverent, and wholly unpredictable—it is highly unlikely that we will ever become a nation of vermouth swiggers in the manner of, say, Argentinians, who make and consume great amounts of vermouth. In Buenos Aires where, by the way, there is a large Italian colony, the cocktail hour is called the "vermouth hour," and afternoon movies are not matinées, but "vermouth features." On the other hand, the wine explosion in the United States has shown dramatically that The Great American Cocktail is not impervious to change. White wine, Kir, spritzers, and other light, vinous libations have made serious inroads into the previously unchallenged position held by the martini, Manhattan, Daiquiri, gin and tonic, Tom Collins, and other standards. And although many drinkers are discovering that a steady diet of white wine is not only monotonous, but if consumed regularly on an empty stomach, without the accompaniment of food, can contribute mightily to the sales position of Tums, Rolaids, and Pepto-Bismol, it is doubtful that they will turn to drinking aperitifs European-style, straight from the bottle. Nor is a mass return to the cocktail-drinking habits of the thirties and forties likely. The logical alternative occupies the middle ground: Wine-based mixed drinks could be the solution, as they are more interesting than wine alone during the cocktail hour but not as authoritative or as deadly as martinis and their ilk.

If this change in happy hour consumption comes to pass, with it will come an entirely new orientation to the cocktail hour. Vermouth, for example, will no longer play a minuscule role in drink-making, as it does today in a twenty-to-one martini. The powerhouse potations will be supplanted by more moderate concoctions, which feature flavor rather than alcoholic strength. While this may not signal the revival of the martini of the Roaring Twenties, which was made with half gin and half vermouth, it will open new vistas for the moderate drinker, who may discover the new world of flavor delights possible when high-proof hookers are *not* the norm. Those of us who grew up in the heyday of The Great American Cocktail will have some adjusting to do, but the new drinkers, who were not weaned on the driest possible mixed drinks, may very well decide they prefer a bourbon Manhattan with considerably more than just a few drops of sweet vermouth.

This, then, is the main thrust of this chapter: Wine-based mixed drinks of moderation, with more emphasis on flavor than on kick. If even a few of these drinks gain popular acceptance, imbibers will be the richer for it. While still enjoying the social stimulation of the happy hour, they will discover new taste experiences, and, perhaps most important, will not make their way to the dinner table glassy-eyed but with clear heads and wide-awake taste buds. A few may again taste food in a way that has not been possible since childhood.

* * *

Because of the vast number of vermouth-related mixed drinks, it is necessary to group them in categories (i.e., vermouth with gin, vermouth with brandy, etc.) to eliminate confusion and duplication of recipes.

Vermouth and Gin Recipes

The *Bronx Cocktail* (essentially vermouth, gin, and orange juice) has been around long enough to have offspring. The modern version is mostly gin, with a dash of orange juice and a few drops of vermouth. Here are some vintage recipes for vermouth lovers.

ᔛ | Bronx Cocktail

1 oz. gin
1 oz. dry vermouth
Juice of a quarter orange
Orange peel

Mix all ingredients except orange peel with cracked ice in a blender. Serve in a chilled cocktail glass. Twist orange peel over drink and drop into glass.

This is also called the *Three Stripes* and *Peter Pan Cocktail*.
A *Golden Bronx Cocktail* is made exactly like a Bronx Cocktail, but with the addition of the yolk of an egg.

ᔛ | Silver Bronx Cocktail

1 oz. gin
½ oz. dry vermouth
½ oz. sweet vermouth
1 oz. orange juice
1 egg white

Mix all ingredients with ice in a blender; strain and serve in a chilled cocktail glass.

For a *Twin Six Cocktail*, omit dry vermouth and add a dash of grenadine.

ᔛ | Bronx Terrace Cocktail

1 oz. gin
1 oz. dry vermouth
Juice of half a lime
Sugar to taste
Maraschino cherry

Mix all ingredients, except cherry, in a blender with cracked ice; strain and pour into a chilled cocktail glass.

This is also called the *Princeton Cocktail*.

The *Zanzibar Cocktail* is similar to the Bronx Terrace Cocktail.

ಇ | *Zanzibar Cocktail*

¾ oz. gin
1½ oz. dry vermouth
1 tbsp. lemon juice
Several dashes of orange
   bitters
Sugar to taste

Mix all ingredients with cracked ice in a blender; strain and pour into a chilled cocktail glass.

And now a procession of vermouth and gin cocktails that use a variety of liquers.

ಇ | *Tuxedo Cocktail*

1 oz. gin
1 oz. dry vermouth
½ tsp. Pernod
Lemon peel

Stir all ingredients, except lemon peel, with ice; strain and pour into a chilled cocktail glass. Twist lemon peel over drink and drop into glass.

Add a dash of Angostura Bitters or maraschino liqueur and you have a *Turf Cocktail*. Add several dashes of grenadine to a Tuxedo Cocktail and you have a *Piccadilly Cocktail*; omit the grenadine and throw in a few dashes of Dubonnet and you have a *Peggy Cocktail*. And if you hanker for an *Imperial Cocktail*, make a Turf Cocktail, but use both Angostura Bitters and maraschino liqueur—but make sure to omit the Pernod.

𝕒 | *Sand-Martin Cocktail*

1 oz. gin
1 oz. sweet vermouth
1 tsp. green Chartreuse
Lemon peel

Stir all ingredients, except lemon peel, with ice; strain and pour into a chilled cocktail glass. Twist lemon peel over drink and drop in glass.

Some beverage historians believe the *Martinez* to be the forerunner of the martini.

𝕒 | *Martinez Cocktail*

1 oz. gin
1 oz. dry vermouth
Several dashes of curaçao
Several dashes of orange bitters
Maraschino cherry

Mix all ingredients, except cherry, in a blender with cracked ice; strain and pour into a chilled cocktail glass. Garnish with cherry.

The Martinez Cocktail also goes under the names of the *Newbury Cocktail* and the *Berry Wall Cocktail*. A variation is the *Orange Bloom Cocktail*, in which triple sec is used in place of curaçao.

𝕒 | *Cat's Eye Cocktail*

1 oz. gin
1 oz. dry vermouth
Juice of 1 lemon
Sugar to taste
Club soda
½ tsp. kirsch

Mix all ingredients, except club soda and kirsch, in a blender with cracked ice; pour into a Collins glass. Fill with soda, stir, and float kirsch on top.

🐚 | Depth Charge Cocktail

1 oz. gin
1 oz. Lillet Blanc
Several dashes of Pernod
Orange peel

Stir all ingredients, except orange peel, with ice; strain and pour into a chilled cocktail glass. Twist orange peel over drink and drop into glass.

Another old standby, the *Darb*, is sometimes called the *Dolly O'Dare Cocktail*. Substitute kümmel for brandy and you have an *Allies Cocktail*.

🐚 | Darb Cocktail

1 oz. gin
1 oz. dry vermouth
1 tsp. apricot brandy
Dash of lemon juice
   (optional)

Mix all ingredients in a blender with cracked ice; strain and pour into a chilled cocktail glass.

Fernet Branca, a pungent bitters and stomachic (digestive stimulant) is made of cinchona, gentian, angelica, myrrh, rhubarb, peppermint, and other botanicals. The *Fernet Branca Cocktail* is sometimes called the *Hanky Panky Cocktail* in old bar guides.

🐚 | Fernet Branca Cocktail

1 oz. gin
½ oz. dry vermouth
½ oz. Fernet Branca
Lemon peel

Mix all ingredients, except lemon peel, in a blender with cracked ice; strain and pour into a chilled cocktail glass. Garnish with lemon twist.

This mixture commemorates Lindbergh's epic transatlantic flight.

Colonel Lindbergh

1 oz. gin
1 oz. Lillet Blanc
1 tsp. orange juice
Several dashes of apricot liqueur

Mix all ingredients in a blender with cracked ice; strain and pour into a chilled cocktail glass.

Tired of dry martinis? Try a *Sweet Martini* for a change.

Sweet Martini

1 oz. gin
1 oz. sweet vermouth
Orange peel
Maraschino cherry

Stir all ingredients, except orange peel and cherry, with ice; strain and pour into a chilled cocktail glass. Garnish with orange peel and cherry.

This delightful potation is a favorite of wine writer William Clifford.

Bill Clifford Special

1½ oz. gin
¾ oz. Chambraise
Lemon or orange peel

Stir gin and Chambraise with ice, adjusting proportions to suit your own taste; strain and pour into a chilled cocktail glass. Garnish with lemon or orange peel.

The following recipe is a little on the sweet side, but then, it is named for a very sweet person.

ès | Carol's Special Cocktail

1 oz. gin
1 oz. sweet vermouth
1 oz. crème de cacao
Egg white
Cinnamon or nutmeg

Mix all ingredients, except cinnamon, in a blender with cracked ice; pour into a large goblet. Sprinkle with cinnamon.

Gin, vermouth, and fruit juices go well together. Here are a trio of zesty cocktails for fruit juice fanciers. The *Palm Beach Cocktail* is also called the *Ideal Cocktail* when dry vermouth is substituted for sweet.

ès | Palm Beach Cocktail

1 oz. gin
¾ oz. sweet vermouth
1 oz. grapefruit juice
Several dashes of
   maraschino liqueur
Maraschino cherry

Mix all ingredients, except cherry, in a blender with cracked ice; strain and pour into a chilled cocktail glass. Garnish with cherry.

ès | Friar Cocktail

1 oz. gin
1 oz. dry vermouth
1 oz. pineapple juice
Maraschino cherry

Mix all ingredients, except cherry, in a blender with cracked ice; strain and pour into a chilled cocktail glass. Garnish with cherry.

ॐ | *Luigi Cocktail*

1 oz. gin
1 oz. dry vermouth
Juice of half a large
   tangerine
Several dashes of grenadine
Several dashes of curaçao

Mix all ingredients with cracked ice; strain and serve in a chilled cocktail glass.

Vermouth devotees often have a passion for mixing dry and sweet vermouth in more or less equal quantities. In the Prohibition era, and before, cocktails like the *Addington* (see chapter I) were to be found in profusion under an assortment of names, but consisting of essentially equal portions of each with minor variations. Here is a sampling.

ॐ | *Vermouth Cocktail*

1½ oz. dry vermouth
1½ oz. sweet vermouth
Several dashes of orange
   bitters

Stir all ingredients with ice; strain and pour into a chilled cocktail glass.

This drink was also known as the *Duplex Cocktail* and the *Neudine Cocktail*, and was sometimes served with a cherry or an orange peel. If you make a Vermouth Cocktail and lace it with a dash or two of maraschino liqueur, you have a *Diplomat Cocktail*, sometimes called a *Cherry Mixture Cocktail*—but don't ask me why. In this case bitters are optional. Omit maraschino and add a dash or two of grenadine and a lemon twist, and you have a *Trocadero Cocktail*. Omit grenadine and add ½ cup orange juice and you have one version of the *Wyoming Swing Cocktail*.

If you introduce gin into the mixing glass along with the vermouth duo, a whole family of recipes appears on the scene. The *Yellow Rattler* is a good example:

🐚 | Yellow Rattler Cocktail

1 oz. sweet vermouth	Mix all ingredients in a blender with
1 oz. dry vermouth	cracked ice; strain and serve in a chilled
1 oz. gin	cocktail glass.
2–3 oz. orange juice	

This drink is also known as the *One Exciting Night Cocktail*; if you omit the orange juice and add a dash or two of Benedictine, you have a *Rolls-Royce Cocktail*. Substitute dashes of brandy, lemon juice, and orange bitters for orange juice and you have a *J.O.S. Cocktail*. If you take a Yellow Rattler Cocktail and add a dash of Grand Marnier and orange bitters, you'll have a *Satan's Whiskers Cocktail*.

*   *   *

Another group of cocktails utilizes equal portions of a combination of vermouths and gin, which may produce a better-balanced drink. The *Trinity Cocktail* is an old favorite.

🐚 | Trinity Cocktail

½ oz. dry vermouth	Stir all ingredients with ice; strain and
½ oz. sweet vermouth	pour into a chilled cocktail glass.
1 oz. gin	

This is also known as the *Polo Cocktail #1*. If you add an ounce of orange juice to the recipe and a dash of Angostura Bitters, you will have a libation that is known, variously, as the *Maurice*, the *Income Tax*, and the *Beauty Spot* cocktails. If you omit the orange juice and add several dashes of orange bitters, you will have the *R.A.C.* (Royal Automobile Club) *Special Cocktail*, sometimes known as the *Smiler Cocktail* or the *Farmer's Cocktail*. Take the R.A.C. recipe and add a teaspoon of white crème de menthe, and *voila!* Before you sits a *Pall Mall Cocktail*. The original recipe specifies equal parts of sweet vermouth, dry vermouth, and gin, but you should feel free to adjust any recipe to your own taste.

Here are some other variations: The *Cooperstown Cocktail* is made exactly like the Trinity Cocktail except that you must add a sprig or two of mint. The *Bloodhound Cocktail*, also known as the *Roma Cocktail*, is a Trinity Cocktail with the addition of three crushed strawberries. The *Queen's Cocktail* is basically a Trinity with a slice of fresh pineapple. And if you would like a *Hotel Plaza Cocktail*, make a Trinity with equal proportions of dry vermouth, sweet vermouth, and gin, then add a slice of fresh crushed pineapple. Here are some others:

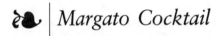 | *Margato Cocktail*

1 oz. light rum
1 oz. dry vermouth
1 oz. sweet vermouth
1 oz. lemon juice
Sugar to taste

Mix all ingredients in a blender with cracked ice; strain and pour into a chilled cocktail glass.

| *Grand Slam Cocktail*

¾ oz. dry vermouth
¾ oz. sweet vermouth
1½ oz. Swedish Punch
  liqueur
Lemon twist

Mix all ingredients, except lemon twist, in a blender with cracked ice; strain and pour into a chilled cocktail glass. Add lemon twist.

Duchess Cocktail

1 oz. sweet vermouth
1 oz. dry vermouth
1 oz. Pernod
Orange peel

Mix all ingredients, except orange peel, with cracked ice in a blender; strain and pour into a chilled cocktail glass. Garnish with orange peel.

This concoction is also called the *Fourth Degree Cocktail*.

Vermouth and Brandy Recipes

Brandy and vermouth make good teammates, as the following recipes will attest. The selection is small due to the fact that many people still look upon brandy as a postprandial drink.

* * *

The *Froupe* is a venerable recipe found in many old mixer's manuals.

Froupe

1½ oz. sweet vermouth
1½ oz. cognac
1 tsp. Benedictine

Stir all ingredients with ice; strain and pour into a chilled cocktail glass.

This is also called the *Rock-a-Bye-Baby Cocktail*.

* * *

The *Charles Cocktail* is another vintage mixture. It is sometimes referred to as the *Metropolitan Cocktail* and the *Young Man Cocktail*, the latter containing several dashes of curaçao.

੨ੂ | *Charles Cocktail*

1½ oz. sweet vermouth
1½ oz. brandy
Dash of Angostura Bitters

Stir all ingredients with ice; strain and pour into a chilled cocktail glass.

If you add a dash of simple syrup to this recipe, it is transformed into a *Harvard Cocktail*. (Why the syrup I'll never know, as it is quite sweet enough without it.) The Charles Cocktail—*sans* bitters—with a dash or two of curaçao or triple sec, becomes the *Queen Elizabeth Cocktail*.

A dry version of the Queen Elizabeth Cocktail is the *Green Room Cocktail*.

੨ੂ | *Green Room Cocktail*

¾ oz. brandy
1½ oz. dry vermouth
½ tsp. curaçao

Stir all ingredients with ice; strain and pour into a chilled cocktail glass.

Here are two more variations on the Charles Cocktail.

੨ੂ | *Presto Cocktail*

1½ oz. brandy
¾ oz. sweet vermouth
1 oz. orange juice
½ tsp. Pernod

Mix all ingredients in a blender with cracked ice; strain and pour into a chilled cocktail glass.

ৰ | *Yanuck Fever Cocktail*

¾ oz. dry vermouth
¾ oz. sweet vermouth
1½ oz. brandy
1 tsp. curaçao
½ tsp. Pernod

Stir all ingredients with ice; strain and pour into a chilled cocktail glass.

The *Gazette Cocktail* is another recipe you will find in all the old drink books.

ৰ | *Gazette Cocktail*

1 oz. sweet vermouth
1 oz. brandy
Juice of half a lemon
Maraschino cherry

Mix all ingredients, except cherry, in a blender with cracked ice; strain and pour into a chilled cocktail glass. Garnish with cherry.

This Roaring Twenties favorite combines vermouth with both brandy and gin.

ৰ | *Victor Cocktail*

1 oz. sweet vermouth
½ oz. brandy
½ oz. gin
Orange peel

Mix all ingredients, except orange peel, in a blender with cracked ice; strain and pour into a chilled cocktail glass. Twist orange peel over drink and drop into glass.

And this is a variation of the Victor Cocktail from the same era.

❧ | Yolanda Cocktail

1 oz. sweet vermouth
½ oz. brandy
½ oz. gin
Several dashes of Pernod
Dash or two of grenadine

Mix all ingredients in a blender with cracked ice; strain and pour into a chilled cocktail glass.

❧ | American Beauty Cocktail

1 oz. dry vermouth
1 oz. cognac
1 oz. orange juice
Dash of white crème de
menthe
1 tsp. ruby port (optional)

Mix all ingredients, except port, in a blender with cracked ice; strain and pour into a chilled cocktail glass. Float port on top, if you wish.

If you make this drink with apricot brandy instead of cognac, it becomes a *Pink Whiskers Cocktail*.

Vermouth and Whiskey Recipes

Vermouth blends as well with whiskey as it does with gin. To its credit, vermouth blends well with both Irish and Scotch whiskeys, which are tricky because of the distinctive malty flavor of Irish whiskey and the peaty taste of Scotch. Here follow some cases in point.

There are several *Shamrock Cocktails* floating around—maybe several hundred, due to the fact that Irish publicans, paying their respects to St. Patrick, come up with new drink recipes every St. Paddy's Day—all called "Shamrocks," naturally. This is one of the better-known concoctions.

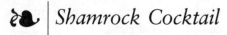 Shamrock Cocktail

1 oz. dry vermouth	Mix all ingredients in a blender with
1 oz. Irish whiskey	cracked ice; strain and pour into a
½ tsp. green crème de	chilled cocktail glass.
menthe	
½ tsp. green Chartreuse	

A variation on the above is called the *Tipperary Cocktail*.

Tipperary Cocktail

1 oz. sweet vermouth	Stir all ingredients with ice; strain and
1 oz. Irish whiskey	pour into a chilled cocktail glass.
1 oz. green Chartreuse	

The *Paddy Cocktail* is another old reliable draught.

Paddy Cocktail

1½ oz. sweet vermouth	Stir all ingredients with ice; strain and
1½ oz. Irish whiskey	pour into a chilled cocktail glass.
Dash of Angostura Bitters	

This drink is sometimes called the *Grit Cocktail*.

The *John Wood Cocktail* is known by various names drawn from the reptile world, such as *Serpent's Tooth* and *Serpent's Smile Cocktail*. Could it be that Mr. Wood was a herpetologist?

❧ | John Wood Cocktail

1½ oz. sweet vermouth
¾ oz. Irish whiskey
¾ oz. lemon juice
1 tsp. kümmel
Dash of Angostura Bitters

Mix all ingredients in a blender with cracked ice; strain and pour into a chilled cocktail glass.

No collection of Irish whiskey and vermouth cocktails would be complete without a *Shillelagh Cocktail*, also known as the *Blackthorn Cocktail*.

❧ | Shillelagh Cocktail

1 oz. dry vermouth
1 oz. Irish whiskey
2–3 dashes of Pernod
2–3 dashes of Angostura
   Bitters

Stir all ingredients with ice; strain and pour into a chilled cocktail glass.

The *Harry Lauder Cocktail*, named for the famous Scottish entertainer, is also an early Rob Roy. It goes by the names of the *Thistle* and the *Flying Scotchman* cocktails as well. Some recipes use simple syrup, but it's not really needed.

❧ | Harry Lauder Cocktail

1½ oz. sweet vermouth
1½ oz. Scotch
Several dashes of
  Angostura Bitters

Stir all ingredients with ice; strain and pour into a chilled cocktail glass.

A variation on the Harry Lauder Cocktail is the *Affinity Cocktail*, which you'll find in most pre-Prohibition bar guides. It is also called the *Whisper Cocktail*.

❧ | Affinity Cocktail

1 oz. sweet vermouth
1 oz. dry vermouth
1 oz. Scotch
Several dashes of
  Angostura or orange
  bitters

Stir all ingredients with ice; strain and pour into a chilled cocktail glass.

Here follows another variation of the Harry Lauder Cocktail, made a mite more interesting by the addition of Benedictine.

❧ | Bobby Burns Cocktail

1 oz. sweet vermouth
1 oz. Scotch
1 tsp. Benedictine

Stir all ingredients with ice and serve in a chilled cocktail glass.

Here are two easy-to-make cocktails, one with pineapple juice and the other with grapefruit juice; or you may want to try orange or lemon juice. All work well in this combination.

🍸 | Wembley #2

1 oz. dry vermouth
1 oz. Scotch
1 oz. pineapple juice
Sugar to taste

Mix all ingredients in a blender with cracked ice; strain and pour into a chilled cocktail glass.

🍸 | Miami Beach Cocktail

1 oz. dry vermouth
1 oz. Scotch
1 oz. grapefruit juice
Sugar to taste

Mix all ingredients in a blender with cracked ice; strain and serve in a chilled glass.

Here are a trio of recipes combining Canadian whiskey and vermouth. The *Scofflaw Cocktail* is from Prohibition days, the others, presumably, are of more contemporary vintage.

🍸 | Scofflaw Cocktail

1 oz. dry vermouth
1 oz. Canadian whiskey
¾ oz. lemon juice
Sugar to taste
Dash of grenadine

Mix all ingredients in a blender with cracked ice; strain and pour into a chilled cocktail glass.

🐌 | Creole Cocktail

1 oz. sweet vermouth
1 oz. Canadian whiskey
2–3 dashes of Amer Picon
2–3 dashes of Benedictine

Mix all ingredients in a blender with cracked ice; strain and pour into a chilled cocktail glass.

🐌 | Canadian Mountie

1 oz. dry vermouth
1 oz. Canadian whiskey
1 oz. Campari
Orange peel

Stir all ingredients, except orange peel, with ice; strain and pour into a chilled cocktail glass. Twist orange peel over drink and drop into glass.

Vermouth and Rum Recipes

Rum and vermouth mixtures form another surprisingly limited category when one considers the vast number of vermouth and gin combinations. The use of light, white rums with vermouth is most rewarding and has produced, among other things, a very acceptable rum martini.

*   *   *

The *Fluffy Ruffles Cocktail* is as basic as you can get, consisting of your favorite rum and sweet vermouth. It is also called the *Little Princess Cocktail*, the *Poker Cocktail*, and the *Havana Club Cocktail*.

🫖 | Fluffy Ruffles Cocktail

1½ oz. light rum
1½ oz. sweet vermouth
Lime or lemon peel

Stir all ingredients, except lime or lemon peel, with ice; strain and pour into a chilled cocktail glass. Twist lime or lemon peel over drink and drop into glass.

The *Palmetto Cocktail* is another oldie. It is also known as the *Trinidad Cocktail*.

🫖 | Palmetto Cocktail

1 oz. dry vermouth
1 oz. light rum
Dash of Angostura Bitters
Lemon peel

Stir all ingredients, except lemon peel, with ice; strain and pour into a chilled cocktail glass. Twist peel over drink and drop into glass.

If you omit the bitters in the Palmetto Cocktail and add a teaspoon of curaçao, you will have a *Country Club Cocktail*.

*   *   *

The *Coronel Batista* is a product of the famed La Flórida Bar, known as the "House the Daiquiri Built" in pre-Castro Havana. Add a teaspoon of apricot brandy and a couple of dashes of grenadine, and it becomes an *Apple Pie Cocktail* or a *Naked Lady*. Take your pick!

૨૰ | Coronel Batista

¾ oz. sweet vermouth
¾ oz. light rum
Juice of 1 small lime or half
   a lemon
Sugar to taste
Maraschino cherry

Mix all ingredients, except cherry, in a blender with cracked ice; strain and pour into a chilled cocktail glass. Garnish with cherry.

And now some odds and ends, all quite different from each other, and all providing some interesting flavor combinations.

૨૰ | Ron Perfecto

¾ oz. sweet vermouth
¾ oz. dry vermouth
1½ oz. light rum
Lemon peel

Stir all ingredients, except lemon peel, with ice; strain and pour into a chilled cocktail glass. Twist peel over drink and drop into glass.

૨૰ | Tango Cocktail

½ oz. sweet vermouth
½ oz. dry vermouth
1 oz. light rum
½ oz. Benedictine
1 oz. orange juice

Mix all ingredients in a blender with cracked ice; strain and pour into a chilled cocktail glass.

🍋 Sunshine Cocktail

1 oz. dry vermouth
1 oz. light rum
1 tsp. crème de cassis
½ oz. lemon juice

Mix all ingredients in a blender with cracked ice; strain and pour into a chilled cocktail glass.

🍋 Jamaica Joy

1 oz. dry vermouth
1 oz. crème de cacao
1 oz. Jamaica rum

Mix all ingredients in a blender with cracked ice; strain and pour into a chilled cocktail glass.

Vermouth and Other Aperitif Wine Recipes

Both sweet and dry vermouths are compatible with other aperitifs, such as sherry and Dubonnet. The mixtures yield some time-tested recipes that are high on the flavor that you come to expect when blending aromatized wines.

*   *   *

Bahia, on the Brazilian coast, boasts one of the most beautiful beaches in the world; perhaps that is why the drink that is named after this lovely old resort is also called the *Brazil Cocktail*.

🕭 | *Bahia Cocktail*

1½ oz. dry vermouth
1½ oz. sherry
½ tsp. Pernod
Several dashes of
   Angostura Bitters

Stir all ingredients with ice; strain and pour into a chilled cocktail glass. (Some recipes specify sweet vermouth, so you may take your choice.)

Another concoction with a South American name is the *Inca Cocktail*—but I have my doubts that the Incas ever tasted one. If you omit the bitters and orgeat syrup, you have a drink known as the *Psychopath*.

🕭 | *Inca Cocktail*

1 oz. sweet vermouth
1 oz. dry vermouth
1 oz. gin
1 oz. sherry
½ tsp. orgeat syrup
Dash of orange bitters

Mix all ingredients in a blender with cracked ice; strain and pour into a whiskey sour glass.

The *B.V.D. Cocktail*, inspired, no doubt, by the men's wear product of the same name, has been around for a long time.

🕭 | *B.V.D. Cocktail*

1 oz. dry vermouth
1 oz. light rum
1 oz. Dubonnet
Orange peel

Stir all ingredients, except orange peel, with ice; strain and pour into a chilled cocktail glass. Twist peel over drink and drop into glass.

There are many *Coronation Cocktails* (see Index). This happens to be one of the better ones. Omit the gin in this recipe and you have a *Merry Widow Cocktail* (see p. 130, this chapter).

🍸 | *Coronation Cocktail #2*

1 oz. dry vermouth
1 oz. gin
1 oz. Dubonnet
Orange peel

Stir all ingredients, except orange peel, with ice; strain and pour into a chilled cocktail glass. Twist orange peel over drink and drop into glass.

Belying its name, the *Soul Kiss Cocktail* is a mild drink that is perfect for cocktail-party imbibing.

🍸 | *Soul Kiss Cocktail*

1 oz. dry vermouth
1 oz. sweet vermouth
1 oz. Dubonnet
1 oz. orange juice

Mix all ingredients with ice in a blender; strain and pour into a whiskey sour glass.

For another version of this drink, try Canadian whiskey in place of sweet vermouth.

*   *   *

There are several Salomes in addition to the dancer, one of which calls for equal parts of gin, dry vermouth, and Dubonnet. The following version is a lighter and perhaps more interesting drink due to the presence of Pernod and the absence of gin; it was named for the original Broadway production of *Salome*.

🙋 Salome Cocktail

1½ oz. sweet vermouth
1½ oz. Dubonnet
½ tsp. Pernod

Stir all ingredients with ice; strain and pour into a chilled cocktail glass.

Vermouth and Assorted Ingredient Recipes

This catchall covey of cocktail recipes with various liqueurs, brandies, bitters, and miscellaneous spirits attests to the versatility of vermouth as a good mixer.

*   *   *

A light, satisfying drink is the *San Francisco Cocktail*, which also goes under the name of the *Sloe Gin Cocktail*.

🙋 San Francisco Cocktail

1 oz. sweet vermouth
1 oz. dry vermouth
1 oz. sloe gin
Dash of orange bitters
Dash of Angostura Bitters

Mix all ingredients with ice in a blender; strain and pour into a chilled cocktail glass.

If you double the portion of sloe gin and leave out the sweet vermouth, you'll have a version of the Blackthorn Cocktail. Substitute sweet vermouth for dry vermouth, and you will have a version of the *Moulin Rouge Cocktail.*

* * *

Yet another version of the Coronation Cocktail specifies applejack or calvados.

ৡ | *Coronation Cocktail #3*

1 oz. sweet vermouth	Stir all ingredients with ice; strain and
1 oz. dry vermouth	pour into a chilled cocktail glass.
1 oz. applejack or calvados	
Several dashes of apricot liqueur	

Here are two more variations on the Coronation Cocktail:

ৡ | *Applejack Cocktail*

1½ oz. sweet vermouth	Stir all ingredients with ice; strain and
1½ oz. applejack or calvados	serve in a chilled cocktail glass.
Dash of Angostura Bitters	

This drink may also be made using dry vermouth in place of sweet.

* * *

According to *Old Waldorf Bar Days*, "Woxum" is an old American Indian word for "raising hell."

| *Woxum Cocktail*

1 oz. sweet vermouth	Stir all ingredients with ice; strain and
1 oz. applejack or calvados	pour into a chilled cocktail glass.
½ oz. yellow Chartreuse	

As we have seen, vermouth blends well with various liqueurs. Here are some representative recipes:

| *Bijou Cocktail*

1 oz. dry vermouth	Stir all ingredients with ice; strain and
1 oz. Grand Marnier	pour into a chilled cocktail glass.
Several dashes of orange bitters	

A drink especially welcome at the end of the work day is the

| *Five-Fifteen Cocktail*

1 oz. dry vermouth	Mix all ingredients in a blender; strain
1 oz. curaçao or triple sec	and pour into a chilled cocktail glass.
1 oz. cream	

ᘒ | *Vermouth-Curaçao Spritzer*

3 oz. dry vermouth
1 oz. curaçao
Club soda
Orange peel

Mix vermouth and curaçao, with ice cubes, in a Collins glass. Fill with soda, stir gently; twist orange peel over drink and drop into glass.

Benedictine, with its complex and intricate flavors, works well in tandem with vermouth. Here are two interesting examples:

ᘒ | *Chrysanthemum Cocktail*

1½ oz. dry vermouth
¾ oz. Benedictine
½ tsp. Pernod
Orange or lemon peel

Stir all ingredients, except citrus peel, with ice; strain and pour into a chilled cocktail glass. Twist peel over drink and drop into glass.

ᘒ | *Tiptop Cocktail*

3 oz. dry vermouth
1 tsp. Benedictine
Several dashes of
    Angostura Bitters
Lemon peel

Stir all ingredients, except lemon peel, with ice; strain and pour into a chilled cocktail glass. Twist lemon peel over drink and drop into glass.

Kümmel has never been very popular in this country. Perhaps it is due to the dominance of caraway flavoring, with overtones of cumin and coriander, which many people associate with food rather than drink. Kümmel is, however, a good mixer and goes well with vermouth. The *Alice Mine Cocktail* also goes by the name of *Scapa Flow Cocktail*.

❧ | *Alice Mine Cocktail*

1 oz. sweet vermouth
1 oz. kümmel
Several dashes of scotch or
   bourbon

Mix all ingredients in a blender with cracked ice; strain and pour into a chilled cocktail glass.

Amer Picon, a bitter cordial made in France, is another spiritous beverage that is used only sparingly in the United States. When mixed with vermouth, however, it makes an interesting drink.

❧ | *Picon Cocktail*

1 oz. dry vermouth
2 oz. Amer Picon
1 oz. gin
Orange or lemon peel

Mix all ingredients, except citrus peel, in a blender with cracked ice; strain and pour into a chilled cocktail glass. Twist peel over drink and drop into glass.

In the *Rose Cocktail*, vermouth softens the rather trenchant flavor of kirsch.

❧ | *Rose Cocktail*

1 oz. dry vermouth
1 oz. kirsch
Grenadine to taste

Mix all ingredients in a blender with cracked ice; strain and pour into a chilled cocktail glass.

The *Lieutenant Colonel Cocktail* was popular at the old Waldorf-Astoria bar in New York City.

ଛ | *Lieutenant Colonel Cocktail*

1½ oz. dry or sweet
  vermouth
1½ oz. Amer Picon
Orange or lemon peel

Mix all ingredients, except citrus peel, in a blender with ice; strain and pour into a chilled cocktail glass.

Maraschino liqueur also goes well with vermouth, as is demonstrated by this tasty libation.

ଛ | *York Special Cocktail*

2 oz. dry vermouth
¾ oz. maraschino liqueur
½ tsp. orange bitters

Stir all ingredients with ice; strain and pour into a chilled cocktail glass.

And finally we will round out our vermouth recipe collection with three tall, satisfying coolers. The *Country Club Cooler* is well established, and is sometimes called the *Roof Garden Cooler*.

ଛ | *Country Club Cooler*

3–4 oz. dry vermouth or
  Lillet Blanc
1 tsp. grenadine or to taste
Club soda or ginger ale
Orange peel cut in a spiral

Put 2 or 3 ice cubes into a 12-oz. Collins glass and add vermouth and grenadine; stir, then fill with club soda or ginger ale. Stir again. Garnish with a long spiral of orange peel.

૨ઙ | *Clover Cooler*

1½ oz. sweet vermouth
¾ oz. sloe gin
3 oz. muscatel wine
Club soda
Lemon peel
Fresh mint sprig

Put 3 ice cubes into a 14-oz. glass and add vermouth, sloe gin, and muscatel; mix with a spoon. Fill with club soda, stir gently, and garnish with lemon peel and mint sprig.

The famous Ritz Bar in Paris has been the wellspring for many a distinguished drink—such as the Mimosa (see chapter I), The *Ritz Fizz* may very well have had its beginnings here.

૨ઙ | *Ritz Fizz*

2 oz. dry vermouth
4 oz. sauterne
½ oz. peach brandy
½ oz. kirsch
½ tsp. orgeat syrup
Club soda
Orange peel cut in a spiral

Put 3 ice cubes into a 14-oz. glass and add vermouth, sauterne, brandy, kirsch, and orgeat; mix well with a spoon. Fill with club soda, stir gently, and garnish with orange spiral.

Of all the fortified, aromatized aperitifs, among the most popular in this country are the quinine-based, flavored wines bearing the names of Dubonnet, Byrrh, and St. Raphael. There are others, such as Pikina, a bitter-orange-flavored aperitif, but you will probably have to take a trip to France to find them. One interesting aperitif that has been made for four hundred years in the Cognac region is Pineau de

Charentes, a partially fermented Charentais white wine to which cognac has been added; it is being sold in the United States under the Reynac brand name. Ratifia is another venerable aperitif made in the famous Champagne district of France, and more recently in California's Napa Valley by the firm of Moët & Chandon. Moët's ratafia is called Panache, and has a pleasant, fruity flavor that is bright and refreshing. Panache is made by adding spirits to pinot-noir grape must, and, I suspect, other assorted herbs and spices. There are others you will find in your travels, some local products, some old and well established, and a few oddments, such as Cynar, an Italian aperitif made from artichokes. For the remainder of this chapter we will confine our approach to artistry with aperitifs to the amusing things that can be done with Dubonnet, Byrrh, and St. Raphael.

Dubonnet is an aperitif success story if there ever was one. It all began in Chambéry, in the Haute Savoie department of France, an area renowned for its wine, where Joseph Dubonnet began blending these wines with his own secret formula for family and friends. Apparently his efforts met with considerable acclaim, for in 1846 he began commercial production in Paris of a red, aromatized wine called, quite naturally, Dubonnet.

It has been suggested that Dubonnet and other quinine-based aperitifs were originally prepared for use in the tropics as antimalarial aids during the time when quinine was the only known medicine to combat this malady. It is more likely that people who spent time in the tropics became used to taking bitter quinine tablets with a swallow of lemonade or wine, and developed a taste for the flavor of cinchona bark, which was satisfied by mixing quinine-flavored aperitifs and soft drinks such as tonic water. In India, gin and Schweppes tonic water was my daily beat-the-heat ritual, but, alas local physicians, well versed in tropical medicine, confirmed the fact that the amount of quinine in a gin and tonic wouldn't have prevented a flea from contracting malaria—it was purely and simply a flavor enhancer.

Whatever the reasons, though, Dubonnet is a marketing as well as an aesthetic success. It has become so popular that it is now made in America and is to be found everywhere in the original red version, Dubonnet Rouge, and the blonde, now called Dubonnet Blanc.

A good way to make the acquaintance of Dubonnet, Byrrh, and St. Raphael is to try some simple, basic drink mixtures. Here are some suggestions. This is one of many versions of the Merry Widow:

₰ | Merry Widow

1½ oz. Dubonnet Rouge	Stir Dubonnet and vermouth with ice;
1½ oz. sweet or dry	strain and pour into a chilled cocktail
vermouth	glass. Twist peel over drink and drop
Orange or lemon peel	into glass.

₰ | Half & Half

1½ oz. Dubonnet Rouge	Stir both Dubonnets together with ice,
1½ oz. Dubonnet Blanc	strain, and pour into a chilled cocktail
Orange or lemon peel	glass. Garnish with peel.

₰ | French Wench

2–3 oz. Dubonnet Rouge	Pour Dubonnet into a Collins glass, add
Ginger ale	2 or 3 ice cubes, and fill with ginger ale;
Lime wedge	stir gently and garnish with lime wedge.

₰ | Swiss Cocktail

2–3 oz. Dubonnet Rouge	Stir with ice, strain, and pour into a
1 oz. kirsch	chilled cocktail glass. Garnish with
Lemon peel	lemon peel.

ARTISTRY WITH APERITIFS

?• | Dubonnet Manhattan

1½ oz. Dubonnet Rouge
1½ oz. blended whiskey
Dash of orange or
  Angostura Bitters

Stir all ingredients with ice; strain and pour into a chilled cocktail glass.

?• | Sherry Dubonnet

1½ oz. Dubonnet Rouge
1½ oz. fino sherry
Lemon peel

Stir Dubonnet and sherry with ice, strain, and pour into a chilled cocktail glass. Garnish with lemon peel.

?• | French Sombrero

1½ oz. Dubonnet Rouge
1½ oz. tequila
Lime or lemon slice

Stir Dubonnet and tequila with ice, strain, and pour into a chilled cocktail glass. Garnish with lime or lemon slice.

?• | Normandy Cocktail

1½ oz. Dubonnet Rouge
1½ oz. calvados
Dash of orange or
  Angostura Bitters
Lemon peel

Stir Dubonnet and calvados with ice, add a dash or two of bitters, strain, and pour into a chilled cocktail glass. Garnish with lemon peel.

The Normandy Cocktail is also known as the *Bentley Cocktail*.

🎵 | *Bushranger*

1½ oz. Dubonnet Rouge
1½ oz. light rum
Several dashes of
  Angostura Bitters

Stir all ingredients with ice; strain and pour into a chilled cocktail glass.

Dubonnet also goes well with fruit juices. Here are three simple, refreshing drinks:

🎵 | *Cranberry Dubonnet*

2–3 oz. Dubonnet Rouge
2–3 oz. cranberry juice
Bitter lemon or lemon-lime
  soda
Mint sprig (optional)

Mix Dubonnet and cranberry juice in a Collins glass with ice cubes. Fill with soda, stir gently, and garnish with mint sprigs, if you wish.

🎵 | *Hawaiian Dubonnet*

2–3 oz. Dubonnet Blanc
3 oz. pineapple juice
Orange soda
Maraschino cherry

Mix Dubonnet and pineapple juice in a Collins glass with ice cubes. Fill with orange soda and stir gently. Garnish with cherry.

🎵 | *Apple Dubonnet*

2–3 oz. Dubonnet Blanc
2–3 oz. apple juice or cider
Club soda
Maraschino cherry

Mix Dubonnet and apple juice in a Collins glass with ice cubes. Fill with soda and stir gently. Garnish with cherry.

While Dubonnet mixes well with many liquors, gin and Dubonnet is the classic combination. In the recipes that follow vodka may be used in place of gin, but the added flavor that gin contributes will be missing in some instances.

ࣾ | *J. P. Fizz*

1½ oz. Dubonnet Rouge	Mix Dubonnet, gin, and curaçao in a
1½ oz. gin	Collins glass with ice cubes; fill with
½ oz. curaçao	soda and stir gently. Twist orange peel
Club soda	over drink and drop in glass. Garnish
Orange peel	with lemon wedge.
Lemon wedge	

The following is a twist on the redoubtable *Negroni* of Italian origins.

ࣾ | *French Negroni*

1½ oz. Dubonnet Rouge	Stir all ingredients, except orange peel,
1½ oz. gin	with ice; strain and pour into a chilled
1½ oz. Campari	cocktail glass. Twist orange peel over
Orange peel	drink and drop into glass.

Here are three favorites from the pre-Prohibition era:

ࣾ | *Opera Cocktail*

1½ oz. Dubonnet Rouge	Stir all ingredients, except orange peel,
1 oz. gin	with ice; strain and pour into a chilled
½ oz. maraschino liqueur	cocktail glass. Twist orange peel over
Orange peel	drink and drop into glass.

This is a variation on the Dubonnet Cocktail. (*See* chapter I).

❧ | *Apparent Cocktail*

1½ oz. Dubonnet Rouge
1½ oz. gin
Several dashes of Pernod

Mix all ingredients with ice; strain and pour into a chilled cocktail glass.

The combination of gin and orange juice is well known, and Dubonnet adds an extra dimension of flavor.

❧ | *Appetizer Cocktail*

1½ oz. Dubonnet Rouge
1½ oz. gin
Juice of half an orange

Mix all ingredients with ice in a blender; strain and pour into a whiskey sour glass.

If you substitute lime juice in place of orange juice in the above, you will have a *Chocolate Soldier Cocktail*.

*   *   *

A variation of the Appetizer Cocktail bears the somewhat sinister name of *Nightmare Abbey Cocktail*.

❧ | *Nightmare Abbey Cocktail*

1½ oz. Dubonnet Rouge
1½ oz. gin
1 oz. orange juice
¾ oz. cherry brandy

Mix all ingredients in a blender with cracked ice; strain and pour into a chilled cocktail glass.

The *Picon Cremaillere* is another old favorite.

👶 | *Picon Cremaillere*

1½ oz. Dubonnet Rouge
1½ oz. gin
1 oz. Amer Picon
Dash of Angostura or
   orange bitters

Stir all ingredients with ice cubes; strain and pour into a chilled cocktail glass.

Byrrh, a proprietary aperitif made from a closely guarded recipe, is also excellent, and of course any mixed drink specifying Dubonnet Rouge can also be made with Byrrh or St. Raphael. Some people prefer to use these aperitifs in place of Dubonnet because they are less sweet, but this is largely a matter of personal taste. Here are some recipes using Byrrh and St. Raphael.

👶 | *Byrrh Cocktail*

2–3 oz. Byrrh
1 oz. gin
1 oz. dry vermouth

Stir all ingredients with ice; strain and pour into a chilled cocktail glass.

The Byrrh Cocktail can be made with blended whiskey, Canadian whiskey, or bourbon in place of gin.

👶 | *Byrrh-Cassis*

1½ oz. Byrrh
1 oz. crème de cassis
Club soda
Orange peel

Mix Byrrh and cassis in a large goblet with ice cubes. Fill with soda, stir gently and garnish with orange peel.

Sirop de citron was a popular flavoring for mixed drinks in the 1920s and before. This recipe comes from that era.

৯৯ | Byrrh-Citron

1½ oz. Byrrh	Mix Byrrh and citron syrup in a large
1 oz. citron syrup	goblet with ice cubes. Fill with soda and
Club soda	stir gently. Garnish with orange peel.
Orange peel	

Here are several fine rum concoctions you might want to try with St. Raphael, which is very similar to Dubonnet and Byrrh in flavor and content.

৯৯ | Dolores Cocktail

2 oz. St. Raphael	Mix all ingredients, except lemon peel,
1 oz. fino sherry	in a blender with cracked ice; strain and
1 oz. Jamaica rum	pour into a chilled cocktail glass. Gar-
Lemon peel	nish with lemon peel.

৯৯ | Capstan Cocktail

2 oz. St. Raphael	Mix all ingredients, except peel, in a
1–2 oz. Jamaica rum	blender with cracked ice; strain and
1 tsp. Grand Marnier or	pour into a chilled cocktail glass.
curaçao	Squeeze orange peel over drink and
Orange or lemon peel	drop into glass.

The name *Opera Cocktail* has been used to identify a number of mixed drinks. This is one of the best ones.

🐌 | *Opera Cocktail #2*

1½ oz. St. Raphael
1½ oz. light rum
Several dashes of lime juice
Orange peel

Mix all ingredients, except orange peel, in a blender with cracked ice; strain and pour into a chilled cocktail glass. Twist orange peel over drink and drop into glass.

There are also several Soul Kiss Cocktails (after all, a provocative name is half the battle). This is number two:

🐌 | *Soul Kiss Cocktail #2*

1 oz. St. Raphael
1 oz. orange juice
1 oz. dry vermouth
1 oz. bourbon

Mix all ingredients in a blender with cracked ice; strain and pour into a chilled cocktail glass.

There are many different recipes for the Soul Kiss Cocktail made with different proportions of bourbon, vermouth, etc. As with all drink recipes, you should have no hesitation about adjusting proportions and adding or deleting ingredients to suit yourself.

*   *   *

And now a few oddments, all good examples of the depth of flavor that Dubonnet, Byrrh, and St. Raphael impart to cocktails.

Mayfair Cocktail

1 oz. Dubonnet
1 oz. cognac
1 tsp. lemon or lime juice
2 dashes of Angostura
    Bitters
Orange peel

Mix all ingredients, except orange peel, in a blender with cracked ice; strain and pour into a chilled cocktail glass. Twist peel over drink and drop into glass.

Dandy Cocktail

1 oz. Byrrh
1 oz. bourbon
1 tsp. Grand Marnier
2 dashes of Angostura
    Bitters
Orange peel

Stir all ingredients, except orange peel, with ice; strain and pour into a chilled cocktail glass.

Pale Moon Cocktail

1 oz. Dubonnet Blanc
1 oz. gin
½ oz. peach brandy
Several dashes of lemon
    juice
Maraschino cherry

Mix all ingredients, except cherry, in a blender with ice; strain and pour into a chilled cocktail glass. Garnish with cherry.

🪶 | *Temptation Cocktail*

1½ oz. St. Raphael
1½ oz. bourbon
1 tsp. Pernod
Lemon peel

Stir all ingredients, except lemon peel, with ice; strain and pour into a chilled cocktail glass. Garnish with lemon peel.

This is named after the lovely Westchester suburb of New York City.

🪶 | *Chappaqua Cocktail*

1 oz. St. Raphael
1 oz. cognac
½ oz. curaçao
½ oz. lime juice
Lemon peel

Mix all ingredients, except lemon peel, in a blender with cracked ice; strain and pour into a chilled cocktail glass. Garnish with lemon peel.

And finally a Canadian entry from beautiful British Columbia.

🪶 | *Vancouver Cocktail*

1 oz. Byrrh
1 oz. Canadian whiskey
1 tsp. lime or lemon juice
Several dashes of orange
   bitters
1 egg white (for two drinks)
1 tsp. Pernod (optional)

Mix all ingredients with cracked ice in a blender, and pour into a large, chilled goblet, adding additional ice if necessary.

The world of aperitif refreshment is colorful, flavorful, and challenging—and largely unexplored by the American drinker. It is also a highly satisfying alternative to the tedium of the "Black Half Hour" at one end of the preprandial spectrum, and the old-time frenetic cocktail hour at the other, when, it seemed, everybody was furiously trying to put away as many strong, straight-up martinis and Manhattans as possible.

The French, who have always excelled at culinary skills, and who have contributed so much to the art of good living, have a wonderful way of describing that most beautiful time of day when the quiet hours of twilight settle upon the land and we put aside our labors to enjoy a period of relaxation before nightfall. They call it *l'heure bleue*, the "blue hour." It is a time for loved ones, for family and friends. And for some, it is a moment for a quiet celebration of life.

It is also the time of the aperitif.

V | HOT DRINKS: CENTRAL HEATING IN A GLASS

Hot wine drinks, laced with various spices, flavorings, and sweeteners, have been quaffed since the days of antiquity. In earlier times, ordinary wine, much of it poorly preserved and well past its prime, was spiced and seasoned to make it palatable—or, in many instances, to provide a welcome change from the deadly sameness of imbibing essentially local wines day after day. In the Middle Ages in Europe, when spices from the Far East provided a ready means of flavor enhancement, new concoctions were made to tempt the palates of the thirsty and grateful multitudes in much the same way as cocktails became the rage five centuries later. Variety is indeed the spice of life.

In the era when the only way to keep warm was to roast in front of the fireplace or snuggle with somebody in bed (a long span that covers most of recorded history), hot drinks were more than simple refreshment; they were "central heating" in a goblet, mug, bowl, tankard, cup, or chalice. In medieval times, spiced wines, whether served hot or cold, were classified as "piments," which is derived from *pigmentarii*, the druggists and herbalists of their day. The best-known drink was called Hippocras, basically a mixture of wine, honey, ginger, cinnamon, and pepper, which became a staple libation throughout Europe. With variations, it is the basis for the modern-day wine mixtures that have become newly popular among skiers and winter sports enthusiasts.

Hot drinks were popular in Colonial America, where spiritous restoratives were considered essential in warding off the chill of winter. Especially important were the curative powers attributed to a wide range of potables made of ale, wine, rum, and brandy. A sturdy punch or a lusty hot grog was believed to be an effective preventive against chills, fevers, plague, ague, "bad vapours and sharp humours."

The taproom—usually the main room of the Colonial tavern—was dominated by a huge fireplace filled with blazing logs. Nearby was the flip iron or loggerhead (sometimes called a "hottle" or "flip dog"), which played a vital part in the preparation of many kinds of hot restoratives. The flip dog was heated to red-hot in the hearth and then plunged into various drink mixtures with much hissing and frothing. The resultant flavor—burnt, bitter, and trenchant—suited the earthy tastes of our Colonial forebears, who reveled in strong drink with fitting names such as "Kill-Divil," "Rattle Skull," and "Whistle-Belly Vengeance." Most of these noxious brews have long since faded into the mists of time, but a few have survived. The flip, a drink made with spirits, beer, eggs, cream, and spices, lives on today, *sans* beer, but is no longer mulled with a red-hot loggerhead. Another hand-me-down is the phrase "being at loggerheads," which, according to lore, is derived from the use of the loggerhead to drive home a point during a heated argument.

There are basic rules in the making of hot, spiritous drinks. Of primary importance is the container you select. For a large gathering, a stockpot with lid is perfect. For smaller groups, a chafing dish is best, for you can prepare your libation in the presence of your guests and keep everything warm throughout the evening. Hot drinks are *never* boiled—not even for an instant—as this not only wastes spirits, which quickly evaporate at high temperatures, but may cause some wines to break down, yielding a decidedly unpleasant burnt flavor. And as much as you prize the handsome silver mugs you won at the company golf tournament, don't use them for piping-hot drinks. Silver, copper, and pewter are excellent heat conductors, and your guests may end up with a severe case of "lip stick" and a few blisters to remember you by. China or earthenware cups are fine—the bigger, the better.

Hippocras, with slight modification to accommodate contemporary tastes, still makes a bracing cold-weather wine punch. This is a basic recipe:

❧ | *Hippocras*

2 liters dry red wine
6 cinnamon sticks, broken
1 dozen whole cloves
1 tbsp. freshly grated ginger
1 tsp. cardamom, cracked
Honey or sugar to taste
Generous grindings of
    nutmeg

Heat all ingredients, except nutmeg, in a large saucepan or chafing dish and bring to a simmer; do *not* boil. Serve in heat-proof mugs and grate nutmeg over each drink.

The original recipe for hippocras often called for a kind of pepper known as "grains of paradise," which has been omitted. Pepper of various kinds was often used in drinks as it was considered a luxury item in medieval times, but now it has been relegated, with a few exceptions, to use in food dishes.

*   *   *

Many modern wine drinks, both hot and cold, are direct descendants of piments—spiced wines—and perhaps one of the most popular, at least throughout Scandinavia, is Glögg (see chapter I). This particular recipe came from a Swedish friend and has proven many times to do that for which it was intended: provide much warmth and cheer on a cold and stormy winter's night. There are many recipes for Glögg, and in Scandinavia nearly every family has a favorite formula. If you live near a store specializing in Scandinavian delicacies, you can probably buy a Glögg mix, consisting of a mixture of dried fruits and spices, but if you have the time, you'll have more fun making your own.

ꙮ | Sven's Glögg

½ gallon dry red wine
1 pint port
½ cup dry vermouth
1 cup blanched almonds
1 cup seedless raisins
¼ cup dried bitter orange
 peel
6 cinnamon sticks
1½ tbsp. cardamom
1 tbsp. whole cloves
1 tsp. aniseed (anise)
1 tsp. fennel seed
⅔ cup sugar or to taste
1 pint vodka
1 pint cognac
1 pint rye

Mix red wine, port, vermouth, almonds, and raisins in a bowl. Fill a cloth bag with orange peel and spices and place in wine mixture; cover and let stand overnight. Pour wine mixture (with spice bag) into a large pot add sugar and heat to simmer for a few minutes, stirring well. Remove from heat and add vodka, cognac, and rye. Return to fire and heat to boiling point; remove bag and pour into chafing dish; cover and keep warm over low heat. Just before serving, remove cover, ignite, and blaze for a moment. Return cover to chafing dish to extinguish flames, and serve with some raisins and almonds in mugs with spoons.

Many spiced wine drinks that are popular today had their origins in ancient Greece and Rome, where, as we have seen, doctoring wines with everything imaginable was a popular pastime. Although modern-day versions employ fewer bizarre additives, tending instead to citrus fruits and distilled spirits of various kinds, the basic formulations have remained essentially unchanged over the centuries. Because of their fuller body, red wines are more popular for hot drinks than white or rosé, although there are a few excellent hot-drink recipes that specify white wines. Some even call for champagne—but this seems to me a waste of good wine, since prolonged heating accelerates the loss of effervescence. (Considering the skill and care needed to get the bubbles into the wine in the first place, why anyone would want to drive them out before a cup has even touched a lip is beyond me! Perhaps these perpetrators are of the same ilk who delight in swizzling their champagne. Better they should attack baser beverages with their swizzlers. Let them expend their efforts on Coke or Pepsi.)

Here follows a selection of hot spiced wine drinks that are as good by the drink as by the bowl. They all are offshoots of hippocras and other venerable potations.

ᐲ | Christmas Punch

2 liters red Burgundy or
  claret
1 lemon, thinly sliced
1 orange, thinly sliced
6 cinnamon sticks, broken
1 tsp. whole cloves
1 cup cognac
1 cup cherry brandy
Honey or sugar to taste

Mix all ingredients in a large saucepan or stockpot and let simmer for 30 minutes, with lid on; do not boil. Transfer to a warmed, heatproof serving bowl or chafing dish and ladle into cups.

ᐲ | English Christmas Punch

2 bottles red Bordeaux
1 fifth (750 ml.) Jamaica or
  gold label Puerto Rican
  rum
Juice of 1 lemon
Juice of 1 orange
3 cups strong tea
Sugar to taste

Heat all ingredients in a large saucepan and simmer for a few minutes, but do not boil. If you wish to flame this punch, fill a large long-handled ladle half full of sugar and cover with rum. Warm ladle in hot punch, ignite, and pour into punch bowl. Then quickly extinguish flames.

🦢 | Cambridge University Punch

2 bottles Beaujolais
1 pint tawny or ruby port
½ pint cognac
1 dozen whole cloves
4 cinnamon sticks, broken
Peel of 1 orange
Honey or sugar to taste

Heat all ingredients in a large saucepan and simmer, but do not boil. Transfer to a chafing dish or warmed, heatproof punch bowl and ladle into cups.

Recipes for *Norfolk Punch* abound in old English drink books. This is one of the best.

🦢 | Norfolk Punch

2 liters red Burgundy
1 fifth (750 ml.) Madeira
1 cup cognac
1 cup curaçao
Zest (outer peel) of 1
    orange
1 tbsp. whole cloves
6 cinnamon sticks, broken
Freshly ground nutmeg
1 pint boiling water
    (optional)

Heat all ingredients, except nutmeg, in a large saucepan and simmer slowly for a few minutes. Transfer to chafing dish or heatproof punch bowl. Ladle into cups and sprinkle with grated nutmeg. Add boiling water to lessen alcoholic strength, if you wish.

Traditionally, *punch* and *cup* mean the same thing. For our purposes, cup is designated as a *single serving* of punch. In theory, any punch recipe may be reduced to an individual serving or cup, and, conversely, any cup should be expandable to a punch. There's just one problem: the same difficulty you encounter when you ask a chef to give you a recipe for two servings from a formulation that was designed for forty people. Not all recipes for either food or drink can be expanded or condensed with the same ratio of ingredients and produce satisfactory results. If you decide to adapt a cup to punch proportions or serve a punch recipe as an individual portion, you are advised to have a dress rehearsal before inviting in guests. Most of these conversions require some adjustments to ensure predictable results.

🐚 | Copenhagen Cup

1½ oz. Peter Heering
3 oz. cherry wine
1 oz. Aalborg aquavit
3 oz. cranberry juice
1 cinnamon stick
3 whole cloves
Orange slice

Heat all ingredients in a saucepan and simmer, but do not boil. Pour into a large heatproof mug.
SERVES 1.

🐚 | Pedro MacDonald's Cup

1½ oz. Scotch whiskey
1½ oz. cream sherry
Dash of Angostura Bitters
Dash of orange bitters
1 tsp. lemon juice
Honey to taste
Cinnamon stick
Orange peel

Heat all ingredients in a saucepan and pour into heatproof mug.
SERVES 1.

🌰 | *Sherry Cup*

4 oz. oloroso or cream
   sherry
1 oz. lemon juice
Dash of Angostura Bitters
Cinnamon stick
3 whole cloves

Heat all ingredients in a saucepan and pour into a heatproof mug.
SERVES 1.

🌰 | *Port Cup*

3 oz. port
1 oz. bourbon
1 oz. dry vermouth
Cinnamon stick
3 whole cloves
Honey to taste
Several dashes of orange
   bitters
Orange peel

Heat all ingredients in a saucepan and pour into a heatproof mug. Add ¼ to ½ cup boiling water, depending upon strength desired.
SERVES 1.

🌰 | *Madeira Cup*

3 oz. Madeira
1 oz. bourbon or cognac
1 oz. dry vermouth
Cinnamon stick
3 whole cloves
Honey to taste
Several dashes of orange
   bitters
Orange peel

Heat all ingredients in a saucepan and add ¼ to ½ cup of boiling water, depending on strength desired.
SERVES 1.

HOT DRINKS: CENTRAL HEATING IN A GLASS

🐚 | *Sherried Cider*

3 oz. oloroso sherry
6 oz. apple cider
1 tsp. lemon juice
Honey (optional)

Heat all ingredients in a saucepan and pour into a heatproof mug. Sweeten with honey if necessary.
SERVES 1.

The flip, a wine drink incorporating eggs, has a long history. It was very much a part of life in the American Colonies, but its popularity in Europe predates the discovery of the New World. The flip is rich, tasty, smooth, and nourishing—everything a fine drink should be—and moreover it is good whether served hot or cold. The Sherry Flip (see Chapter I) is a classic wine drink. It was very popular during Victorian times and the Roaring Twenties. As everything goes in cycles, the flip, in its many manifestations, will no doubt be "discovered" on a college campus and once again become the rage.

🐚 | *Port Flip*

3 oz. port (you may also
    use Madeira, Marsala, or
    a Burgundy or
    Bordeaux)
1 egg
1 tsp. sugar
2 oz. heavy cream
Freshly grated nutmeg

Heat wine in a saucepan, but do not boil. In a bowl beat egg with sugar, using a whisk or beater. Blend in cream with egg; pour in warm wine and stir well. Serve in mug and sprinkle with nutmeg.
SERVES 1.

The eggnog is but a variation of the flip and may be enjoyed either hot or cold. The secret to a successful eggnog is to separate the eggs, beat yolks and whites individually, and then carefully fold (not beat) whites into the yolks.

🐦 Wine Eggnog

1 dozen eggs, separated
1½ pints heavy cream
1 lb. sugar
1 liter port
1 pint cognac
1½ pints milk
Freshly grated nutmeg

Beat yolks to a froth; slowly stir in cream and sugar. Gradually add wine and cognac, stirring constantly. Beat egg whites and fold into mixture. Ladle mixture into mug until half full. Heat milk and fill mugs to top. Stir gently; grate nutmeg on top and serve immediately. (*Note*: Milk should not be too hot or eggs will curdle.)

The Tom and Jerry, the perennial Christmas-season favorite, is basically a hot wine eggnog that can be made with hot water in place of milk or cream. Here is a variation on the traditional recipe, which is usually made with Jamaica rum and bourbon or brandy.

🐦 Tom and Sherry

1 dozen eggs, separated
½ lb. sugar
1 tbsp. each cinnamon, allspice, and cloves
4 oz. Jamaica rum
1 fifth (750 ml.) cream sherry
Hot water or milk
Freshly grated nutmeg

Beat yolks and whites separately. Beat sugar and spices into yolks; mix in rum gradually. Gently fold in whites. Ladle mixture into mugs until half full. Add 2 oz. sherry and fill with hot water. Top with nutmeg.

Back in the days of "wooden ships and iron men," grog was basically a watered rum ration. This precursor of the highball and myriad spirits on the rocks was reputedly named for Adm. Edward

Vernon, who won the sobriquet "Old Grog" for his ubiquitous grogram cape and instituting the practice of cutting the rum ration, issued to sailors of the Royal Navy, with water. Capt. Henry Morgan, the scourge of the Spanish Main, had the foresight to add fresh lime juice to his ship's grog ration, presumably to prevent scurvy among the crew. This practice had an ancillary benefit: It greatly improved the flavor and, perhaps, laid the foundation for a whole new generation of rum drinks. Nowadays the term "grog," applies to drinks of every description—with and without rum and other strong spirits. In fact, more often than not it is used to describe a hot libation. And wine drinks are no exception.

Lemon Wine Grog

3 oz. claret or Burgundy
Juice of 1 small lemon
Sugar to taste
Lemon twist
Boiling water

Mix all ingredients, with a little boiling water, in a large mug until sugar is dissolved, then fill with boiling water. SERVES 1.

Mulled Madeira

4 oz. Madeira
½ oz. Cointreau
Juice of half a lemon
Orange peel
Boiling water
Honey (optional)

Mix all ingredients, except honey, with a little boiling water, in a mug until well blended; then fill with boiling water. Add honey if more sweetness is desired.

Hot buttered rum is a famous grog with many desirable qualities, especially for butter lovers. Hot buttered wine? A friend in California sent in a recipe for hot buttered California muscatel wine to be served as a party drink with butter and maple syrup and a good dash of boiling water. You may want to try a variation, named, appropriately enough, the *Butter Cup*.

₴ | *Butter Cup*

4 oz. Malmsey Madeira
1 oz. cognac
Dash of triple sec
Boiling water
Lemon twist
1 pat of butter
Freshly grated nutmeg

Heat wine, cognac, triple sec, and several ounces of water until simmering, but do not boil. Pour into a large mug, fill with boiling water, and stir. Add lemon and butter, dust with nutmeg.

Here is another buttery grog for apple knockers.

₴ | *Hot Apple Grog*

Half a baked apple
4 oz. amontillado sherry
1 oz. calvados or applejack
1 cinnamon stick
Pinch of ginger
Pinch of nutmeg
3 whole cloves
2 oz. apple cider
Sugar (optional)
1 pat of butter
Lemon slice

Place baked apple in a large mug. Heat sherry, calvados, spices, and cider in a saucepan. Add sugar, if needed, and stir well. Bring to a simmer and pour steaming into mug. Add pat of butter and lemon slice.

That redoubtable company of "libations of the Cloth" (otherwise known as bishops) were great favorites in the pre-central-heating era. The English have always revered the tart flavors of citrus fruits, especially since they combine readily with every kind of wine and spirit, and the bishop is basically a roasted orange or lemon, with or without spices, combined with hot wine. The *English Bishop* is probably the best known (see chapter I), but there are others, and they make interesting hot drinks, especially when a chill is in the air. By its nature, the bishop is a festive drink, and was especially popular at Christmastime, as Charles Dickens relates in *A Christmas Carol*. You will no doubt recall this happy scene after Ebenezer Scrooge finally got religion.

"A merry Christmas, Bob!" said Scrooge, with an earnestness that could not be mistaken, as he clapped him on the back. "A merrier Christmas, Bob, my good fellow, than I have given you for many a year! I'll raise your salary, and endeavor to assist your struggling family, and we'll discuss your affairs this very afternoon, over a Christmas bowl of smoking bishop, Bob! Make up the fires, and buy another coal-scuttle before you dot another i, Bob Cratchit!"

🐦 | *Lemon Bishop*

2 large lemons
Whole cloves
½ tsp. each of mace, allspice, cinnamon, and ginger
1 fifth (750 ml.) ruby port
1 cup water
6 sugar cubes
Lemon peel

Stud one of the lemons with several dozen cloves and bake or roast it until it is heated through. Cut this lemon into quarters and place in a saucepan with spices, port, and a cup of water and bring to a boil. Rub the other lemon briskly with sugar cubes until they become saturated with zest (outer peel) and oil. Add sugar cubes to pan and stir until dissolved. If you want a "smoking bishop" you can flame it for a few seconds, but it's not necessary.

There are other variations of the bishop. For example, when oranges are left to stand in the wine for a day or so, and the juice is then pressed out of them and reheated, the resulting drink becomes a "Bishop à la Prusse." If a bordeaux wine is used in place of the traditional port, it is called a "cardinal." If a bishop is made with port and tea, it is demoted and called a "churchwarden." A bishop may not be made with apples for then the drink becomes a Wassail. Although we have yet to encounter a recipe for a bishop incorporating tangerines or grapefruit, in our searching through many eighteenth- and nineteenth-century writings on the subject of food and drink, it engenders warm thoughts and may just be worth a try.

Another hot drink category popular in merry old England is the posset. The posset is simply a mixture of milk, sweetened and spiced and curdled with ale or wine; eggs are sometimes used, with or without milk. The posset is a very bracing drink after a day on the ski slopes. A time-tested recipe for an egg posset is given in Chapter I. A typical wine posset recipe utilizing white wine such as a chardonnay, Chablis, or Graves follows. This is one of the rare times when a hot drink recipe calls for boiling ingredients.

ಕ್ಲ | *Wine Posset*

1 quart milk	Boil milk and wine together in a saucepan until milk curdles. Strain the whey and put the curds aside. Blend sugar and lemon peel into the whey. Press curds through a sieve and beat into the whey. Sprinkle with spices and serve in preheated mugs.
Generous ½ pint white wine	
Sugar to taste	
Lemon peel, grated	
½ tsp. each of ginger, cinnamon, and nutmeg	

The *Sack Posset*—sack being the term for sherry that was a part of the popular usage of the day—was a great favorite in the eighteenth century. This fine old recipe for a *Snow Posset* made with sack comes from *The Complete Family-Piece*, a homey compendium of all aspects of country living, containing practical remedies for common maladies as well as extensive sections on food and drink preparation. This recipe, published in London in 1739, is just as serviceable today as it was when it was written.

TO MAKE A SNOW POSSET

Take a Quart of new Milk, and boil it with a stick of Cinnamon and quartered Nutmeg; when the Milk is boiled, take out the Spice, and beat the Yolks of sixteen Eggs very well, and by degrees mix them in the Milk till 'tis thick; then beat the Whites of sixteen Eggs with a little Sack and Sugar into a Snow; then take the Bason you design to serve it up in, and put in it a Pint of Sack; sweeten it to your Taste; set it over the fire, and let one take the Milk, and another the White of Eggs, and so pour them together into the Sack in the Bason; keep it stirring all the while 'tis over the Fire; when 'tis thorough warm, take it off, cover it up, and let it stand a little before you use it.

The *Ale Posset*, as it is sometimes called, is yet another variation of this drink from ancient times. Sir Walter Raleigh's recipe for his favorite posset is simple and good.

🐌 | *Sir Walter Raleigh's Posset*

½ pint full-bodied English ale
½ pint medium sherry
1 quart milk
Sugar to taste
Freshly grated nutmeg

Heat ale and sherry in a saucepan to the boiling point, but do not boil. Gradually stir in hot milk that has also been brought to the boiling point. Sweeten to taste and serve in mugs with grated nutmeg.

And now a final, very rich recipe. Perfect for holiday festivities, the *Pope's Posset* could almost double for a dessert.

𝒆𝒂 | The Pope's Posset

¾ lb. blanched almonds,
   slivered
1 cup water
1 pint oloroso sherry
Sugar to taste
Freshly grated nutmeg
Cinnamon

Beat almonds, adding a little water to make a smooth consistency, until creamy as butter. Place almond paste in saucepan and heat with a cup of water. Stir in sherry; blend well. Add sugar and sweeten to taste. Serve hot in cups with spoons and sprinkle with nutmeg and cinnamon.

The restorative power of a properly made hot wine drink is well known. When you feel that you are about to succumb to a winter's chill, croup, ague, grippe, or "bad vapours," it is time to schedule an early evening and to have a go at the famous "double-hat treatment." This recipe comes from Maestro Karoly Zesdeny, a Hungarian who ultimately found Chile's climate more agreeable than that of Transylvania.

𝒆𝒂 | The Double-Hat Remedy for Cold and Flu

1 cup red Burgundy or Egri
   Bikaver Hungarian red
   wine
4 oz. cognac
1 tsp. honey or to taste
3 whole cloves

Heat wine to boiling point in a saucepan; add cognac, honey, and cloves; simmer for a few minutes, but do not boil. Pour into a mug that has been scalded with boiling water. Place your hat on a chair at the foot of the bed, then get into bed. Sip wine mixture; do not let it get too cool. When you can see two hats on the chair, you're on the road to recovery.

VI | A FORTIFIED WINE FORMULARY

The scene is a walnut-paneled dining room in a stately English country house in Kent or Surrey. The men are in dinner jackets, and the ladies are wearing long gowns that shimmer in the soft light of crystal sconces and silver candelabra. Liveried footmen gliding noiselessly about the guests have cleared the table of the last vestiges of *crème brûlée à l'orange*. At one end of the long table, the hostess arises and with a gracious smile says, "Ladies, let us adjourn to the drawing room for our demitasse and leave the gentlemen to their cigars and port." We follow the men to a well-appointed billard room, the walls covered with armorial trappings, trophies of the hunt, and framed photographs of various masculine exploits in faraway places; the gentlemen light long Montecristos, supplied by the host, and pour glasses of port from gleaming, cut-crystal decanters.

The scenario is a familiar one to moviegoers who, after viewing repeated episodes of bewigged actors sipping their postprandial port, sherry, and Madeira in various period pieces, have become thoroughly convinced that the drinking of these great wines is a ritual that went out of style with hoop skirts, gaslights, and horsedrawn carriages. Fortunately for those who enjoy the niceties of life, a revival of sorts has begun to take shape that may bring fortified wines back into the realm of everyday usage. This renaissance may include after-dinner drinking, but its main thrust will be mixed drinks, not merely sipping an aged sherry or a crusted port with the accompaniment of a Havana cigar by the fireside, however romantic and appealing that may seem. Besides, today's woman is not going to retire meekly from the party and indulge in "girltalk" over a cup of coffee; she will jolly well stay with the men and enjoy the after-dinner festivities—which might even include puffing on a cigar, it it's really a good one.

The great company of fortified wines, which includes not only the big three—port, sherry, and Madeira—but such Mediterranean delights as Malaga, from the Costa del Sol of Spain, and Marsala, from the Sicilian seaport of the same name, as well as other lesser wines, has long had a dedicated following in England and other parts of Europe. Until recently the United States has been a big consumer of imported ports, sherries, and Madeiras, but the demand has been declining as traditional drinkers grow older and are replaced by new generations of young consumers raised on sweet specialty wines, flavored wines, and, more important, good, inexpensive, readily available California, New York State, French, Italian, and Spanish table wines of the "jug" type. Of great significance is the fact that this new wave of drinkers are innovators. They don't drink brandy from a snifter, but they will mix it with grapefruit juice; they will not sip port with their coffee after dinner, but they will mix it with blackberry brandy and have it on the rocks. They may not drink a fino sherry as an aperitif in the manner of their grandmothers, but many learn early the difference between a well-made sherry and the cheap, tawdry pseudo-sherries that are popular on skid row because of their relatively high alcoholic content. They are not connoisseurs in the traditional sense, but they are creative experimenters, interested in exploring new flavor combinations.

Port and blackberry brandy may not be your favorite cocktail, but it is not far removed from the port and cognac concoctions that were popular in Georgian England. Some of these new drinkers will graduate to the aficionado level and join the ranks of those who savor a vintage port or an old Madeira. Along the way, many new drink recipes will be generated. Some will become popular with all age groups and sweep the country. A few will become classics and join the ranks of Kir, the French 75, sangría, the champagne cocktail, the sherry flip, Black Velvet, and other established favorites. New ways will be found to enjoy the distinguished family of fortified wines, not as portrayed in Hollywood historical-romantic epics, but as everyday, staple refreshments enjoyed for their own inherent qualities as cocktails, coolers, punches, and party drinks. The purpose of this chapter is to present a broad sampling of libations, old and new, that will provide some insight into the many interesting recipe possibilities with port, sherry, and Madeira.

Fortified wines, as differentiated from table wines, have a higher alcoholic content, ranging from 15 to 21 percent, and, with few exceptions (as in the case of certain ports so exceptional that they are declared a "vintage" and designated by the year of their harvest) they are all blends of various years. These wines are designated by the United States government as "dessert wines," a somewhat restrictive classification since sherries, particularly, have long been enjoyed before as well as after meals. For our purposes here, we will call them "cocktail wines" as that is their function. Again, as mentioned in our discussion on champagne mixtures, we will not be using vintage ports, venerable Madeiras, and expensive sherries for mixed drinks—but neither will we be using cheap, domestic jug sherries, ports, muscatels, and similar low-cost dessert wines, which are an embarrassment to the majority of the skilled and dedicated American wine-makers who strive to turn out quality products. Again, the level of quality you settle upon for mixed drinks is a matter of personal taste, and in some cases personal finances. Here, since we are primarily concerned with results, you are urged to explore the great middle ground of quality fortified wines, both imported and domestic. There are those who will order a whiskey sour and take whatever bar whiskey the bartender happens to use. Others will specify a blended whiskey or a medium-priced Canadian. Then there are some who will insist that their sour be made with an aged Kentucky bourbon. If you care about flavor and want predictably good results in wine mixed drinks, you needn't use the very best, but you shouldn't use the very worst, either, just because a wine is being blended with other ingredients. Remember what every chef knows: You cannot depend on a combination of good flavors to mask one bad one. A poor wine used in a beef stew tends to degrade all of the other ingredients that you have used in your recipe.

Sherry is made in the south of Spain in an area known as the "Sherry Triangle" situated in a delimited area around Jerez de la Frontera, extending to Puerto de Santa María to the south and to Sanlúcar de Barrameda to the west. The very driest of the dry sherries come from Sanlúcar de Barrameda. It is known as *manzanilla*. It has been described as having an aroma of ripe apples and a hint of salt air. It has the lowest alcoholic content of all the sherries, 15 percent by volume. You will not find too much of this around on dealers' shelves, as it is too dry for most palates. (However, a martini-drinking friend swears by it, claiming it makes a far drier martini than any vermouth in existence.) *Fino* is light, dry, and very fragrant and is best served chilled. It is a favorite accompaniment with *tapas*, the bar nibbles and appetizers the Spanish love with their sherries. *Amontillado*, which Edgar Allan Poe made famous in his classic horror story, is amber-colored; it is usually full-bodied and medium dry and has a pleasantly nutty flavor and bouquet. *Oloroso* is imbued with the great classic sherry taste: full-bodied, mellow, often on the sweet side, with a rich bouquet reminiscent of walnuts. *Cream* sherries are the sweetest of the lot, as the name suggests. They are rich, full-bodied, and mellow at their best, with a dark color, and are dessert sherries in the truest sense of the word. Good sherries are available in the United States at very competitive prices at this writing since the demand has fallen off in recent years. It is hoped that this is a temporary cyclical turn of events as these fine wines deserve greater popularity. Also, since World War II, American vintners have been making some exemplary sherry-type fortified wines worthy of serious investigation by wine connoisseurs.

Port, a sweet, rich wine named for the city of Oporto, comes from the Douro region in northern Portugal. The Douro, a mountainous area that has been a wine-growing center from Roman times, was designated as a demarcated district by the Portuguese government in 1756. This means that no wine of a similar type can be properly labeled port unless it is made in the Douro area from grapes grown in this delimited zone. Obviously, there are many port-type wines made in the United States, and some of the California ports are quite good. Unfortunately, almost any kind of red wine can be called port in this country, so the Portuguese government adopted the designation *porto* in 1968. This means that only fortified wines from the Douro may be called *porto* and marketed as such in the United States.

Port has long been a great English favorite, and for two hundred years it has been the official wine used for toasts by the British royal family as well as by other dignitaries of English officialdom. So, when you see a historical film in which the regimental commander at the head of the dinner table, resplendent in his bemedaled mess jacket, rises, glass held high, to propose a toast, "To the Queen," you may be absolutely certain that that goblet holds port, or a reasonable facsimile thereof.

The most common type of port is *ruby*. It is rich, fruity, with great depth of flavor, and, as the name indicates, is a dark, ruby red. *Tawny* port is matured longer than ruby and as a consequence loses much of its red color and becomes a pale brown. It is mellower than ruby and more costly. *White port* is made in the same way as its cousins, but of different grape varieties. It is not considered to be in the same class with red grape ports and is generally looked upon as a poor relation by the wine trade. Once in a while the wine from a particular harvest is so outstanding it is designated as a *vintage port* and is allowed to mature, unblended. Vintage ports fetch high prices and some may take as long as fifty years to reach their prime; if good common sense does not deter one from using a vintage port in a mixed drink, the stiff price should be sufficiently discouraging. Another premium unblended port is known as *late-bottled vintage port*, which is kept in the barrel about twice as long as vintage port (hence the term *late-bottled*), matures faster, and is generally not of the same exceptional quality as a true vintage port. However, these are excellent buys for laying down for the short term, and, even though they are not in the vintage category, it would be a pity to use them for cocktails and punches when there is such an abundance of good rubys and tawnys, all blended, of course, at very nominal prices. Ports have an alcoholic content that ranges between 19 and 21 percent and thus will remain sound at room temperature* for an extended period of time after being opened, unlike lower-proof table wines.

The fortified wines from Madeira, the tiny island far out in the Atlantic, some 360 miles west of the coast of North Africa, were immensely popular in Colonial America. Today, even though many Madeiras have flavor characteristics found in no other wine and are endowed with elements of true greatness, very little Madeira is shipped to this country. Madeiras are popular in England and northern Europe and especially in France, where chefs consider it to be a cooking wine unlike any other. Unlike in the United States, in European kitchens wines used in cooking are accorded considerable respect, and no professional chef would use a wine in a food dish that he didn't consider drinkable.

Madeira, like sherry, is made by the *solera* system, a blending technique by which young wines are carefully combined with older wines in successive stages to achieve a consistently good quality of wine, year after year. As with sherry, there are no vintage wines bottled. Dates on Madeira labels do not signify a vintage wine, but rather the date of the wine from the earliest *solera*, which may comprise but a very small part of the many wines from succeeding years that have been used to make up the blend. The unique, and frequently intense, flavor of many Madeiras is due in part to the fact that these wines are "baked" for a number of months in warming ovens called *estufas*, which promote rapid maturation. At certain stages during the vinification process, the wine is fortified with wine spirits, usually brandy. The fortification process, the timing of which is precisely determined by the cellarmaster, stops the fermentation at a point considered desirable, depending upon the type of Madeira being made. A dry Madeira such as a *Sercial* will be fortified only after a considerable amount of sugar has been transformed to alcohol by fermentation. A sweet Madeira such as a *Malmsey* will be fortified early in the vinification process. Early or late, all Madeiras are eventually brought up to 18 to 20 percent alcohol by volume. In the days of sailing ships, fortification had an ancillary benefit: It enabled the wines to ship well over rough

---

* "Room temperature," a phrase often encountered in old wine books, is not American room temperature (70° to 80°F.) but English or European room temperature (55° to 60°F.).

A FORTIFIED WINE FORMULARY

seas and in torrid climates. It is said that the *estufa* method of maturing Madeiras evolved as a means of duplicating the seasoning that these wines received in the holds of ships on long sea voyages.

Sercial, the driest Madeira, is pale gold or amber, with a pronounced bouquet; it is made from the Sercial grape. It is frequently served as an aperitif, like fino sherry. *Verdelho* has a richer color and is a bit sweeter than Sercial. "Rainwater," a name coined by an American importer in Savannah, Georgia, during the era when Madeiras were all the rage, was synonymous with Verdelho Madeiras. Now the term is used broadly to denote any pale, medium-dry Madeira. *Boal* or *Bual* Madeiras are rich, golden in color, and quite sweet. The sweetest of all the Madeiras, and a true dessert wine, is *Malmsey* (from the Malvasia grape, hence the anglicized name), which ranges from deep golden amber to rich brown in color and possesses a full bouquet and fine, rich flavor and character. At its best, it offers a superb taste experience, and it is a shame that it has fallen out of favor with all except a few very perceptive wine lovers. If fortified wines ever come into fashion again in America (as I strongly suspect they will), Malmsey will surely be a most sought-after wine.

Marsala is a fortified wine made in the vicinity of the Sicilian seaport of the same name. Marsala was developed by English wine merchants in the eighteenth century as an inexpensive substitute for ports and sherries, which were then at the height of their popularity in England. Admiral Nelson is said to have fortified the British Navy with it, and apparently with some success, since Britannia was certainly the undisputed ruler of the waves during this era. The Marsala that is usually exported to this country is labeled *Superior*, and although available sweet or dry, the sweet variety is the most common. Marsala *fini* is the lightest and least expensive. *Vergini* is dry and is made by the *solera* system in the manner of Madeiras and sherries. Various flavored Marsalas known as *Speciale* may contain egg, quinine, or various fruit extracts. Marsalas range in alcoholic strength from 17 to 20 percent and have a pronounced flavor that makes them well suited for food dishes.

Another popular fortified wine made in Sicily, southern Italy, and the islands of Sardinia and Pantelleria is *Moscato* (muscatel). These are considered dessert wines due to their high sugar content. All are fortified (15 to 17 percent alcohol) and have the sweet, characteristic flavor of the Muscat grape.

Two Spanish fortified wines, not well known in the United States but sometimes encountered by travelers to Spain, are *Malaga* and *Tarragona*. Malaga is a sweet, rich red wine produced near the city of Málaga on Spain's famed resort area, the Costa del Sol. It is made by the *solera* system and fortified. Tarragona is another sweet, red wine, also known as *Priorato* in Spain. It is made around the city of Tarragona on the Mediterranean coast about sixty miles south of Barcelona. Although little is shipped to the United States, these, like other of the lesser fortified wines, have distinctive qualities and can be used as the basis for some unusual wine drinks. Those who travel in wine-producing countries and who have an inquisitive palate may chance upon fortified wines that are unknown outside of their immediate areas. Some are worth bringing home for use as dessert wines, but more importantly, for the qualities they and all other fortified wines impart to punches and various other mixed drinks; good mixers all because of their strength, staying power, and intense flavor and bouquet.

Any old-time mixer's manual that contains a goodly number of pre-Prohibition drink recipes will attest to the popularity of sherry as a cocktail ingredient. Perhaps the renaissance of sherries, ports, and Madeiras will, at least in the United States, follow in the path that has been blazed by a mixed drink that sweeps the country. This has indeed been the making of many a spiritous beverage that was propelled to fame by a mixed drink that suddenly caught the public fancy. What the Moscow Mule did for vodka and the Kir did for crème de cassis may very well bring sherry to the fore. The recipe may be in this collection, or we may have to await the arrival of an ingenious mixologist to create it. Whatever the future may hold, one thing is certain: Fortified wines contribute to the making of some very delightful wine drinks.

*   *   *

Here is a selection of basic sherry mixed drinks that have enjoyed varying degrees of popularity over the years.

❧ | Sherry Manhattan

3 oz. fino sherry
½ oz. sweet vermouth
1 tsp. grenadine (optional)
Orange peel

Stir spirits with ice, strain, and pour into a chilled cocktail glass. Twist orange peel over drink and drop into glass.

❧ | Sherry Sour

Juice of half a lemon
Sugar to taste
3 oz. fino sherry
Maraschino cherry

Mix lemon juice, sugar, and sherry (you may use a medium sherry, if you wish) in blender with ice. Serve in a whiskey sour glass. Garnish with cherry.

❧ | Sherry and Ginger

3 oz. medium sherry
10-oz. bottle ginger beer

Prechill sherry and ginger beer and mix gently in a large, chilled goblet. It is best when served very cold.

❧ | Cupid Cocktail

4 oz. medium sherry
1 egg
Sugar to taste
Pinch of cayenne pepper

Mix all ingredients, except pepper, in a blender with ice; pour into a chilled goblet. Sprinkle with pepper.

🐚 | *Sherry Mist*

4 oz. medium sherry
Several dashes of raspberry
  syrup

Fill a wineglass with shaved or finely crushed ice. Pour in sherry and raspberry syrup and stir.

This is a variation on the Cupid Cocktail. The idea is not to break the egg, but gulp it, and the sherry, down together. Not for everyone, to be sure.

🐚 | *Sherry and Egg*

1 egg
Medium sherry

Place raw egg in a whiskey sour glass and fill with sherry. Take care not to break the egg. Chilling the sherry beforehand may help.

An old classic, this. The name *Xeres* is the French word for sherry. If you don't have any orange bitters, use Angostura Bitters instead.

🐚 | *Xeres Cocktail*

3–4 oz. amontillado sherry
Orange bitters to taste
Lemon peel

Fill a double old-fashioned glass with ice cubes; pour in 3 to 4 oz. sherry and as many dashes of orange bitters as you like. Stir and add lemon twist.

This is an old favorite that dates from Grandmother's day, and beyond. This is one of the "original" recipes, but feel free to vary the sherry-vermouth ratio to please your tastes.

ੈ੨ Adonis Cocktail

3 oz. fino sherry
1 oz. sweet vermouth
Dash of orange bitters

Stir all ingredients with ice; strain and serve in a chilled cocktail glass.

The *Pruneaux Cocktail* originally called for prune syrup, which has gone out of vogue along with syrup of figs and cod liver oil. Prune juice will do just as well.

ੈ੨ Pruneaux Cocktail

2 oz. dry sherry
2 oz. gin
1 oz. prune juice
1 oz. orange juice
Orange peel

Mix sherry, gin, and fruit juices in a blender with cracked ice. Serve in a chilled goblet and garnish with orange peel.

Another old gin-and-sherry mixture is the *Roc-a-Coe*, which was originally garnished with a cherry. Modern tastes would opt for a lemon twist.

ੈ੨ Roc-a-Coe Cocktail

1½ oz. gin
1½ oz. medium sherry
Lemon peel

Stir gin and sherry with ice, strain, and serve in a chilled cocktail glass. Garnish with lemon twist.

Wine lemonades have been popular for many years and are equally good whether made with sherry, port, Madeira, or a robust red table wine.

ૐ | *Sherry Lemonade*

Juice of 1 lemon
Sugar to taste
3–4 oz. sherry
Club soda
Maraschino cherry

Mix lemon juice and sugar in a Collins glass until sugar is dissolved. Stir in sherry, add ice cubes, and fill glass with club soda. Add cherry.

The *East Indian Cocktail* is another oldie from the time when mixed drinks were less dry. Adjust proportions to your taste.

ૐ | *East Indian Cocktail*

1½ oz. dry vermouth
3 oz. oloroso sherry
Dash of orange bitters

Stir or shake all ingredients with plenty of cracked ice; strain and pour into chilled cocktail glass.

The Rickey, originally made with gin, was named for Col. Joe Rickey, a famous, old-time Washington lobbyist.

ૐ | *Sherry Rickey*

Juice of 1 lime
Sugar to taste
3–4 oz. medium sherry
Club soda

Mix lime juice and sugar in a highball glass until sugar is dissolved. Stir in sherry, add ice, and fill with club soda.

Table wines blended with sherry make refreshing coolers and tall drinks. Here is a sampling:

🐌 | *Velvet Blush*

4 oz. sauterne
2 oz. oloroso sherry
Lemon peel

Mix sauterne and sherry in a Collins glass with ice and garnish with lemon peel. If more sweetness is desired, add sugar or use a cream sherry.

🐌 | *Sherry Hawaiian*

2 oz. dry sherry
4 oz. dry white wine
Juice of half a lemon or 1
   lime
2 oz. pineapple juice
Sugar to taste
Pineapple slice (optional)
Maraschino cherry
   (optional)

Mix all ingredients, except pineapple slice, in a blender with cracked ice; pour into a 12-oz. Collins glass. Garnish with pineapple or a maraschino cherry.

🐌 | *Rhinelander Cooler*

3 oz. Rhine or Mosel
2 oz. fino sherry
¾ oz. triple sec or
   maraschino liqueur
Juice of 1 orange
Juice of half a lime
Several dashes of orange or
   Angostura Bitters
Club soda

Mix all ingredients, except club soda, in a blender with ice; pour into a 12-oz. Collins glass. Fill up with cold club soda and stir gently.

From Andulusia comes this fine tall drink.

🙣 | Cadiz Cooler

1½ oz. fino sherry
1 oz. Spanish brandy or
   cognac
½ oz. curaçao or triple sec
Tonic water
Orange slice

Mix sherry, brandy, and curaçao in a blender with cracked ice. Pour into a Collins glass and fill with tonic. Garnish with orange slice.

Sherry's affinity for brandy is to be expected inasmuch as the same grape varieties that go into the making of sherry are used to produce some very excellent Spanish brandies. Here are a bevy of sherry sippers' delights with special appeal for brandy bibbers.

🙣 | Sherry Twist Cocktail #1

2–3 oz. medium sherry
1 oz. Spanish brandy or
   cognac
1 oz. dry vermouth
1 oz. curaçao
Several dashes of lemon
   juice
Cinnamon (stick or
   ground)

Mix all ingredients, except cinnamon, in a blender with cracked ice; strain and pour into a chilled whiskey sour glass. Garnish with cinnamon stick or sprinkle ground cinnamon over drink.

Flamenco Cocktail

1½ oz. dry sherry
1 oz. brandy
1 oz. white rum
¾ oz. triple sec or simple
    syrup to taste
Dash of Angostura or
    orange bitters
Lemon peel

Mix all ingredients, except lemon peel, with cracked ice in a blender; strain and pour into a large, chilled stemmed glass. Garnish with lemon peel.

Torero

1½ oz. oloroso sherry
1 oz. Martinique or
    Jamaica rum
¾ oz. heavy cream
Sugar to taste
Dash of Angostura Bitters
    (optional)

Mix all ingredients in blender with cracked ice; strain and pour into a chilled cocktail glass. If a cream sherry is used, omit sugar.

In the world of cocktail names there are many *Valencias* and *Havanas*. Here are two of the best.

Valencia

1½ oz. fino sherry
1½ oz. applejack or
    calvados
Several generous dashes of
    orange juice

Mix all ingredients in a blender with cracked ice; strain and pour into a chilled cocktail glass.

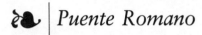

Havana

¾ oz. cream sherry
1½ oz. amber rum
3–4 dashes of lemon juice
Orange peel

Mix all ingredients, except orange peel, in a blender with cracked ice; strain and pour into a chilled cocktail glass. Squeeze orange peel over drink and drop into glass.

Puente Romano (meaning "Roman bridge") is named for a beautiful resort hotel built around the remains of an old Roman bridge, near the town of Marbella.

Puente Romano

2 oz. cream sherry
1½ oz. orange juice
¾ oz. brandy
1½ oz. heavy cream
Dash of curaçao

Mix all ingredients in a blender with cracked ice; strain and pour into a chilled whiskey sour glass.

For those who enjoy rich drinks, here are a few that will send your bathroom scales into orbit.

Sherry Shake

½ pint butter pecan ice
   cream
4 oz. milk or half-and-half
1 ripe banana
4 oz. medium sherry
Dash of amaretto
Freshly grated nutmeg

Mix all ingredients, except nutmeg, in a blender at slow speed until slushy, or beat with an egg beater. Pour into chilled double old-fashioned glasses and serve with grated nutmeg on top. SERVES 2.

A FORTIFIED WINE FORMULARY

🐌 | Dublin Sherry Eggnog

1 egg
2–3 oz. oloroso sherry
1–2 oz. Bailey's Original
  Irish Creme Liqueur
Several dashes Irish
  whiskey
4–6 oz. milk
Freshly grated nutmeg

Prechill all ingredients; mix everything, except, nutmeg in a blender; pour into a tall chilled Collins glass. Grate nutmeg on top.

🐌 | Sherry Ramos Fizz

2 tbsp. lemon juice
1 tsp. lime juice
2 tbsp. heavy cream
1 egg white
3 oz. cream sherry
Sugar to taste
½ tsp. orange flower water
Club soda
Powdered sugar

Prechill all ingredients and mix everything, except club soda and powdered sugar, in a blender or shaker with a scant cup of cracked ice. Moisten the rim of a large wineglass with lemon juice and coat by rolling in powdered sugar. Pour in mixture and fill glass with soda.

And now a roundup of sherry drinks, old and new, designed for a wide range of tastes.

🐌 | Sherry Screwdriver

6 oz. fresh orange juice
2 oz. medium sherry
1 oz. vodka
½ oz. curaçao

Mix all ingredients in a blender with cracked ice and pour into a double old-fashioned glass.

This is one of several *Coronation Cocktails* (see Index).

❧ | Coronation Cocktail #1

3 oz. sherry
2 oz. dry vermouth
Several dashes of
 maraschino liqueur
Several dashes of orange
 bitters

Stir all ingredients with cracked ice; strain and pour into a chilled cocktail glass.

The *Philomel Cocktail* is taken from the Greek for nightingale. Who knows, a few of these may put you in good voice!

❧ | Philomel Cocktail

3 oz. sherry
1 oz. light rum
2–3 oz. orange juice
Several dashes of Pernod

Mix all ingredients in a blender with cracked ice; strain and pour into a chilled goblet.

❧ | Cork Cooler

1½ oz. Irish whiskey
1–2 oz. fino sherry
½ oz. sweet vermouth
Dash of Pernod
Club soda
Lemon peel

Stir all ingredients, except soda and lemon peel, in a Collins glass with several ice cubes. Fill with soda and add lemon peel.

≿❧ | *Stone Cocktail*

2 oz. sherry
1 oz. white rum
½ oz. sweet vermouth
Lemon peel

Stir all ingredients, except lemon peel, with cracked ice; strain and pour into a chilled cocktail glass. Garnish with lemon peel. If you prefer a drier drink, switch proportions for rum and sherry.

≿❧ | *Moss Rose*

3 oz. fino sherry
4–6 oz. grapefruit juice
1 oz. sloe gin

Mix all ingredients in a blender with ice; pour into a chilled double old-fashioned glass.

≿❧ | *Sherry Twist Cocktail #2*

3 oz. medium sherry
1½ oz. bourbon
1 tbsp. triple sec
2–3 oz. orange juice
Several dashes of lemon
    juice
2–3 whole cloves
Pinch of cayenne pepper

Mix all ingredients in a blender with cracked ice; strain and pour into a chilled whiskey sour glass.

≿❧ | *Stephen's Cocktail*

1 oz. medium sherry
1 oz. dry vermouth
1 oz. Benedictine

Mix all ingredients in a blender with cracked ice; strain and pour into a chilled cocktail glass.

In case you've been imbibing a number of the foregoing sherry-based cocktails, here are two mixtures that employ both sherry and port to help you make the transition to libations based on red fortified wines.

🍷 | Iberian Club Cocktail

1½ oz. dry sherry
1½ oz. tawny port
Several dashes of orange
   bitters

Stir all ingredients in a mixing glass with cracked ice; strain and pour into a chilled cocktail glass.

🍷 | Port Splash

2 oz. medium sherry
1 oz. Spanish brandy or
   cognac
Several dashes of simple
   syrup or curaçao
½ oz. ruby port

Mix sherry, brandy, and syrup or cura-çao in a blender with cracked ice; strain and pour into a chilled cocktail glass. Float port on top.

In Georgian England, the nobility esteemed port, along with Madeira, and, to a lesser degree, brandy; gin, ale, beer, porter, and stout were the standard liquid fare of the so-called working classes. Cocktails, as such, had yet to be invented, but wine mixtures were popular in the eighteenth century in the form of punches, the Negus, the syllabub (which could be a drink or a dessert; see chapter I); and spirits, primarily brandy, mixed with fortified wines, especially port.

Here follow some port potations, in the spirit, if not the style of the Age of Reason, modified for modern tastes.

Some recipes for this drink actually call for coffee. Even if you're a coffee addict, we don't recommend it.

è | *Coffee Cocktail*

1½ oz. ruby port
1½ oz. brandy
Sugar to taste
1 egg (for two drinks)
Freshly grated nutmeg

Mix all ingredients, except nutmeg, in a blender with cracked ice; strain and pour into a chilled cocktail glass. Sprinkle with nutmeg.

Coffee Flip is made exactly as above except for the addition of a tablespoon of milk or half-and-half.

* * *

The *Port Flip* is a classic wine drink, mild and nourishing, and long popular as a tonic for the aged and infirm.

è | *Port Flip*

2–3 oz. port
1 egg
Sugar to taste
Freshly grated nutmeg

Mix all ingredients, except nutmeg, in a blender with cracked ice; strain and pour into a whiskey sour glass. Sprinkle with nutmeg.

The *Devil's Cocktail* is an old one dating from the days when it was made with equal parts of dry vermouth and port. A more contemporary drink results when you use less vermouth.

🐌 Devil's Cocktail

2 oz. ruby port
¾ oz. dry vermouth
Juice of half a small lemon
Several dashes of Grand
   Marnier (optional)

Mix all ingredients in a blender with cracked ice; strain and pour into a chilled cocktail glass.

This is an original in the Georgian spirit—but with a very contemporary name.

🐌 Port Snort

1½ oz. tawny port
1½ oz. sloe gin
Maraschino cherry

Mix port and gin in a blender with cracked ice; strain and pour into a chilled cocktail glass. Garnish with a cherry.

Chicago's Imperial House has gone to restaurant heaven, but in its day, it was perhaps the loftiest citadel of haute cuisine in the Windy City. The use of egg yolks instead of whole eggs gives this bracer, a specialty of the Imperial House, its distinctive touch.

🐌 Imperial House Bracer

3 oz. port
2 oz. brandy
2 egg yolks
1 oz. sweet cream
Freshly grated nutmeg

Mix all ingredients, except nutmeg, in a blender with cracked ice; strain and pour into chilled cocktail glasses. Sprinkle with nutmeg.
SERVES 2.

A FORTIFIED WINE FORMULARY

Another old favorite that was originally made with equal parts port and brandy is the *Betsy Ross*. If you prefer a drier drink, increase the amount of brandy.

₹**ℯ** | *Betsy Ross*

1½ oz. brandy	Stir well in a mixing glass with ice
1 oz. port	cubes; strain and pour into a chilled
½ oz. curaçao	cocktail glass.
Dash of Angostura Bitters	

The *Philadelphian* is one of several good cocktails employing calvados or applejack in combination with port.

₹**ℯ** | *The Philadelphian*

2 oz. ruby port	Mix all ingredients in a blender with
2 oz. calvados or applejack	cracked ice; strain and pour into a
2 oz. orange juice	chilled whiskey sour glass.

Substitute an ounce of lemon juice for orange juice, a little sweetening and throw in an egg and you turn the Philadelphian into a *Country Cocktail*.

*   *   *

Depending upon how keen you are about blackberry brandy, feel free to adjust the proportions of this cocktail to suit your taste.

₹**ℯ** | *Poop Deck Cocktail*

1½ oz. tawny port	Mix all ingredients, except lemon peel,
¾ oz. brandy	in a blender with cracked ice; strain and
¾ oz. blackberry brandy	pour into a chilled cocktail glass. Gar-
Lemon peel	nish with lemon peel.

This potation doesn't really look like chocolate, it certainly doesn't taste like chocolate, and it surely doesn't act like chocolate. Why it was named the *Chocolate Cocktail* we don't know—and for that matter, don't really care.

🐦 | *Chocolate Cocktail*

2–3 oz. port ¾ oz. yellow Chartreuse 1 egg yolk Sugar to taste	Mix all ingredients in a blender with cracked ice; strain and pour into a chilled cocktail glass.

Another chocolate drink *sans* chocolate:

🐦 | *Chocolate Daisy*

1½ oz. port 1½ oz. brandy Juice of half a lemon 1 tsp. raspberry syrup or grenadine	Mix all ingredients in a blender with cracked ice; strain and pour into a chilled cocktail glass.

Here are a couple of fizzes that were popular back in the days when seltzer was squirted out of syphon bottles.

🐦 | *Chicago Fizz*

1½ oz. port 1½ oz. Jamaica rum Juice of half a lemon 1 egg white Sugar to taste Club soda	Mix all ingredients, except club soda, in a blender with cracked ice; pour into a Collins glass. Add ice cubes and fill with soda.

🍃 Japanese Fizz

1½ oz. port
1½ oz. bourbon or blended
  whiskey
Juice of half a lemon
1 egg white
Sugar to taste
Club soda

Mix all ingredients, except club soda, in a blender with cracked ice and pour into a Collins glass. Add ice cubes and fill with soda.

This is one of several *Princeton Cocktails* (see Index).

🍃 Princeton Cocktail #2

1 oz. ruby port
1½ oz. gin
Several dashes of orange
  bitters

Mix all ingredients in a pitcher with cracked ice; strain and pour into a chilled cocktail glass.

This is a variation of an old Louisiana plantation recipe.

🍃 Creole Punch

Juice of 1 lime or small
  lemon
Juice of 1 medium orange
3 oz. ruby port
1½ oz. brandy
Falernum or simple syrup
  to taste
Dash or two of Angostura
  Bitters
Water or club soda

Mix all ingredients, except soda, in a blender with cracked ice; pour into a 14-oz. cooler or Collins glass. Add more ice if necessary, fill with a little water or club soda, and stir.

Port coolers have long been popular due to the fact that the distinctive flavor of port and Madeira stands up quite well to other ingredients as well as to the chilling effect of ice-cold drinks on the taste buds.

Any Port in a Storm

Juice of 1 lemon
3–4 oz. ruby port
1 oz. brandy
½ oz. maraschino liqueur
Club soda

Mix all ingredients, except club soda, in a blender with cracked ice; pour into a 12-oz. Collins glass. Add several ice cubes and fill with soda.

The *Porto Alegre Cooler* is a fine hot weather drink, named after the busy Brazilian seaport.

Porto Alegre Cooler

2–3 oz. tawny port
1½ oz. bourbon
½ oz. sweet vermouth
Juice of 1 lime
Several dashes of orange
   bitters
Simple syrup

Mix all ingredients, except club soda and syrup, in a blender with cracked ice and pour into a Collins glass; fill with soda. If additional sweetening is needed, add simple syrup.

There are a host of drinks named for, or purported to come from, Sloppy Joe's, that famous Havana bar of the pre-Castro era. This is one of them.

A FORTIFIED WINE FORMULARY

🍸 | Sloppy Joe's Cocktail

1 oz. ruby port
2 oz. cognac
3 oz. pineapple juice
Several dashes of curaçao
Several dashes of grenadine

Mix all ingredients in a blender with cracked ice; strain and pour into a chilled whiskey sour glass. Adjust proportions to suit your taste.

This is named after the merchant princes of the British wine trade.

🍸 | Bristol Baron

1½ oz. tawny or ruby port
1½ oz. Grand Marnier
Several dashes of orange
  bitters
Several dashes of
  Angostura Bitters

Mix all ingredients in a blender with cracked ice; strain and pour into a chilled cocktail glass.

The Algarve is the Riviera of southern Portugal and the origin of this tasty cooler.

🍸 | Algarve Punch

3–4 oz. dry white port
1 oz. gin
¾ oz. sweet vermouth
½ oz. Pernod
Club soda
Lemon peel

Stir all ingredients, except soda and lemon peel, in a pitcher with ice and pour into a highball or Collins glass. Add ice cubes, fill with soda, and twist lemon peel over drink and drop into glass.

Our collection of port potations wouldn't be complete without a couple of oddballs.

₹₳ | *Veracruz Cocktail*

1½ oz. tequila
1 oz. ruby port
Dash of curaçao
Lemon peel

Stir all ingredients, except lemon peel, with ice; strain and pour into a chilled cocktail glass. Add lemon peel.

₹₳ | *Alto Douro Cocktail*

2–3 oz. ruby or tawny port
1½ oz. apricot brandy
Lemon peel

Stir all ingredients, except lemon peel, with ice; strain and pour into a chilled cocktail glass. Add lemon peel.

In many of the foregoing recipes, Madeira, Marsala, and similar red fortified wines may be substituted for port. Here is a small sampler of Madeira and Marsala mixed drinks.

₹₳ | *Madeira Cooler*

1½ oz. Madeira
1½ oz. cognac
Juice of 1 lime
1 oz. passion fruit juice
1 oz. pineapple juice
Dash of Angostura Bitters
Orange slice
Pineapple stick

Mix all ingredients, except orange and pineapple in a blender with cracked ice and pour into a 12-oz. Collins glass. Garnish with orange slice and pineapple stick.

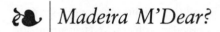

❧ Sicilian Sling

Juice of half a lime
Dash of Angostura Bitters
1½ oz. gin
1–2 oz. Marsala
Simple syrup to taste
Club soda
Benedictine (optional)

Mix all ingredients, except club soda and Benedictine, in a blender with cracked ice; pour into a 12-oz. Collins glass. Add additional ice if necessary, fill with soda, stir gently, and carefully float Benedictine on top with a teaspoon.

There is only one answer to this question: Yes!

❧ Madeira M'Dear?

1½ oz. Madeira
1½ oz. bourbon
Juice of half a lemon
½ oz. curaçao
Orgeat or simple syrup to taste

Mix all ingredients with cracked ice in a blender; strain and pour into a chilled cocktail glass.

❧ Playa del Rey

1–2 oz. Madeira
1 oz. cognac or Spanish brandy
½ oz. curaçao
Lemon peel

Mix all ingredients, except lemon peel, in a blender with cracked ice; strain and pour into a chilled cocktail glass. Garnish with lemon peel.

🎀 | Baltimore Eggnog

1 egg
¾ cup milk
2 oz. Madeira or Marsala
1 oz. Jamaica rum
½ oz. apricot brandy
Sugar to taste
Freshly grated nutmeg

Mix all ingredients, except nutmeg, in a blender with cracked ice; strain and pour into a Collins glass. Sprinkle with nutmeg.

🎀 | Dooley's Dram

1½ oz. Irish whiskey
1–2 oz. Madeira or
    Marsala
¾ oz. amaretto
1 oz. lime or lemon juice
Orange peel

Mix all ingredients, except orange peel, in a blender with cracked ice; strain and pour into a whiskey sour glass. Twist orange peel over drink and drop into glass.

🎀 | Madeira Milk Punch

2–3 oz. Madeira
1 oz. vodka
¾ oz. white crème de cacao
¾ cup milk
Cinnamon or freshly grated
    nutmeg

Mix all ingredients, except cinnamon or nutmeg, in a blender with cracked ice; strain and pour into a large highball glass. Sprinkle with cinnamon or nutmeg.

ව | Funchal Flip

2–3 oz. Madeira
1 egg
Sugar to taste
Freshly grated nutmeg

Mix all ingredients, except nutmeg, in a blender with cracked ice; strain and pour into a chilled cocktail glass.

If you've managed to come this far in sampling some of the many delights that are contained in this fortified wine formulary, you should feel confident in your ability to meet—and master—any situation that may arise, no matter how bizarre or unexpected. For example, you are a guest at dinner in a stately English country house in Kent or Surrey and the hostess arises and with a gracious smile says, "Ladies . . . and gentlemen, let us all adjourn . . . not to the drawing room for demitasse, but to our well-appointed billard room, where we have something special planned. Not what you think. Not a billard match, but rather a drink-mixing contest using our ample supply of sherries, ports, Madeiras, and other diverse fortified wines. Shall we go?" On the pretext of going to the Gents', you steal off to the library, where only that morning, with your tea, you happened to spot a soiled copy (wine spots, of course) of *this very book*. You pluck it off the shelf and with trembling hands leaf through it quickly until you come to *this very chapter*. You scan it eagerly by the light of a solitary lamp on the library table. You pick out a half dozen recipes that you know, from your hard-won experience as a mixologist, are simply smashing. Thus armed, you carefully replace the book, turn out the light, and very slowly and quietly open the library door and peer up and down the hall. The coast is clear, as they say, so you scurry off to join the others.

The drink-mixing contest is already under way as you enter the well-appointed billard room, the walls covered with armorial trappings, trophies of the hunt, and framed photographs of various masculine exploits in faraway places. The air is blue with a haze generated by some of the guests nervously puffing away on their long Montecristos, which, you perceive, are being supplied by the host. The hostess, between puffs, calls out your name. The time has come, but you are confident. You are prepared. You are undaunted by the fact that the sideboard is awash with a plethora of some rather formidable-looking potations. You reach for various ingredients and magnanimously announce the fact that you will enter not one, but *three* drink entries: one with sherry, one with port, and one with Madeira. Applause. The host comes over and shakes your hand. "That's the spirit I like. I, too, entered a recipe in each category."

The judging is quickly conducted on a blind basis (numbers substituted for the names of contestants) by the local publican and his two barmaid daughters, the cook, the gamekeeper, the gardener, and the village greengrocer. The winner? None other than the host—and he placed first in all three categories. You are stunned, but you smile bravely as the host speaks. "Ladies and gentlemen. I am deeply honored, but I have a confession to make. No, the contest wasn't rigged, but I did have an advantage that I consider unfair. I boned up this morning by reading a book in my library that is concerned with the making of fine wine drinks. Therefore I am withdrawing and giving my prize, a case of rare 1945 vintage port, to the runner-up. The envelope, please." The cook hands him an envelope, which is opened after considerable fumbling. The host glances at the paper, his face lights up, he turns and points to *you*! "Jolly good show, old boy! Come forward and receive your well-earned prize." As the guests crowd around the sideboard, eager to sample the winning drinks, the host continues to pump your sweaty hand and pat you on the shoulder. You are clearly the man of the hour in his eyes. But you must blurt it all out. You, too, must make a clean breast of things. It is hard to find the right words. "I say, sir"—your voice is raspy—"I, too, boned up. I had a look at your wine drink book." Your host smiles avuncularly. "I know, old chap, I saw you slip into the library after dinner. I guessed what you were there for." Your host senses your embarrassment. "Not to worry," he says grandly. "You beat me fairly, and at my own game. The prize is yours. As one of your American writers once said, 'Opportunity benefits he who is best prepared,' and you, sir, *were prepared*, eh what!"

And that is precisely the purpose of this little book—to prepare you to make prize-winning wine drinks.

APPENDIX: PRIMARY INGREDIENTS

APPENDIX: PRIMARY INGREDIENTS

APPENDIX: PRIMARY INGREDIENTS

INDEX